The Battle for Fallujah

by Chief Warrant Officer 4 Timothy S. McWilliams, with Nicholas J. Schlosser

Introduction:
The First Battle for Fallujah

In the spring of 2003 a United States-led Coalition invaded Iraq and deposed Saddam Hussein's Baath regime. Over the course of the next eight years the United States faced a persistent, multifaceted insurgency dedicated to expelling American forces from Iraq and destroying the new American-sponsored government created to replace Saddam's regime. In the course of its struggle to stabilize and defend the nascent Iraqi government, the U.S.-led Coalition fought two battles in 2004 to secure the city of Fallujah. The first battle was fought in April. Launched in retaliation for the murder of American contractors by insurgents, the assault sparked a public outcry that led an anxious and still embryonic Iraqi civilian government to order an end to the battle just days after it had begun. The suspension of operations left the city in insurgent hands. Several months later, the United States launched a second battle to clear the city. This second battle, known variously as the Second Battle of Fallujah, Operation Phantom Fury, and Operation al-Fajr, began in November 2004 and ended with the city cleared and under Coalition control by the end of December of that year. This is a study of that second battle.

The anti-U.S. insurgency that erupted in the summer of 2003 was waged by a variety of groups, ranging from former regime loyalists to foreign Islamist organizations such as al-Qaeda. While these groups had different membership make ups, diverse motivations, and were shaped by a range of ideologies, they were all dedicated to ousting the United States and Coalition from Iraq and destroying the U.S.-supported Iraqi government. Fallujah was a center of insurgent activity. As with the western al-Anbar Province as a whole, the city was dominated by tribal society and was often too volatile for even the Baath regime to effectively govern. The United States did not find administering the city any easier. On 28 and 30 April 2003, for instance, U.S. soldiers in the city from the 82d Airborne Division, besieged by a mob, killed 13 and wounded 91 civilians. The action inflamed anti-American attitudes and set the tone for operations in the city over the course of the following year. U.S. and Coalition forces struggled to bring security and stability to the city, but by March of 2004 it remained a volatile and dangerous place outside effective U.S. and Iraqi control.[1]

That same month, the U.S. Army 82d Airborne Division transferred occupation duties in al-Anbar Province to the I Marine Expeditionary Force (I MEF). The Marine air-ground task force, which included the 1st Marine Division, 3d Marine Aircraft Wing, and 1st Force Service Support Group, had participated in Operation Iraqi Freedom the previous year. Shortly after it had returned to the United States in the fall of 2003, it was readied for a second deployment to Iraq.

To prepare for its deployment to al-Anbar, I MEF's ground combat element commander, Major General James N. Mattis, set about indoctrinating the 1st Marine Division in the practices and principles of counterinsurgency. The Marines would approach the security problem in Iraq differently than the Army had. They would patrol through the city streets, develop combined units integrating Marines and Iraqi soldiers, and try and cast a different image to the Iraqis than the so-called heavy-handed Army had done. This approach, Mattis and his superior, Lieutenant General James T. Conway, believed, would strengthen relations between the Americans and Iraqis and separate the insurgent forces from the general population. The Marines would focus on defeating the insurgency, not insurgents.[2] By the end of March 2004, I MEF had assumed full responsibility for security in al-Anbar from the 82d Airborne Division.

The 1st Marine Division deployed its two regiments along the Euphrates River. Regimental Combat Team 7 was given responsibility for the province's west while Regimental Combat Team 1 took control of the province's eastern areas. Among the urban areas under Regimental Combat Team 1's jurisdiction was Fallujah.

On 31 March 2004, four contractors from the Blackwater security firm entered the city of Fallujah in two sport utility vehicles. They did not inform the local Marine headquarters that they would be doing so (despite injunctions on unauthorized travel in the city) and thus the Marines were unable to protect the contractors when their vehicles were ambushed and destroyed. The contractors were all killed by an angry mob, and their bodies hung along the King Faisal Bridge which spanned the Euphrates in Fallujah's western section. Footage of the burnt, mutilated bodies of Americans hanging behind irate crowds were broadcast by the cable news station al-Jazeera and subsequently beamed by news outlets across the world.[3]

1

On 31 March 2004, four contractors from Blackwater International were ambushed and killed by insurgent forces in Fallujah. Their bodies were subsequently mutilated and hung on this bridge in Fallujah, pictured here in 2008.

Among the many shocked by the images were the members of the George W. Bush administration, who immediately put pressure on the Coalition headquarters in Iraq—Combined Joint Task Force 7 led by Lieutenant General Ricardo S. Sanchez, USA—to launch a retaliatory mission against the insurgents in the city. On 3 April 2004, Sanchez ordered I Marine Expeditionary Force to conduct an offensive operation—codenamed Operation Vigilant Resolve—against the city. Both General Conway and General Mattis protested the order, arguing that a large-scale operation would send the wrong message, unnecessarily endanger civilians, and ultimately fail to achieve the primary objective of locating the individuals responsible for the murders. Their protests were overridden and I MEF launched an assault on the city.[4]

Over the course of six days, three Marine battalions from Regimental Combat Team 1 commanded by Colonel John A. Toolan Jr. established a cordon around the city and then began a slow and methodical advance into the city. The fighting against insurgents was fierce, and enemy forces utilized every structure in the city for cover, in-cluding mosques, as they fought the Marines. When one of these was destroyed, the story spread that the Marines had deliberately killed civilians, though no evidence existed supporting the claim. Stories such as these worried the still nascent Iraqi Governing Council. Subsequent insurgent uprisings in ar-Ramadi and an-Najaf were further points of concern, and the Iraqi leaders began to pressure the head of the American occupation authority, L. Paul Bremer, to end the battle. On 9 April 2004, Coalition headquarters ordered I Marine Expeditionary Force to suspend all offensive operations in Fallujah.[5]

The United States carried out Operation Vigilant Resolve in a state of confusion. Lacking a cohesive psychological operations plan, the Coalition was quickly outmaneuvered by insurgent propaganda. Although the Marines took great care to utilize artillery and air strikes as selectively as possible, there were civilian casualties, with an estimated 220 Iraqi civilians killed during the first two weeks of the fighting. Insurgent propaganda organs subsequently exploited these events and characterized the Marine offensive as excessively brutal and heavy-handed. The Coalition also

Battle for Fallujah

faced a mutiny from Iraqi forces attached to the 1st Marine Division who refused to advance into the city.

The Marines' hard-fought tactical gains were also undermined by a series of miscalculations that ultimately led to Fallujah becoming an insurgent base of operations for al-Anbar Province. Bremer's hope to pass authority from the Coalition Provisional Authority to the Iraqi civilian government as quickly as possible prompted him to acquiesce to the council's demand to suspend the offensive operation. Hoping to maintain pressure on the city but also put an Iraqi face on the battle, General Conway gambled on an all-Iraqi force, known as the Fallujah Brigade, led by a former Baath general. This force, Conway hoped, would be able to better stabilize the city and help reduce the impression that only the United States was interested in clearing the city of insurgent forces. The brigade ultimately failed, however, with many of its members joining the insurgency.[6]

In the summer of 2004, al-Anbar Province remained unstable. Marines in Regimental Combat Team 7 had fought a series of engagements along the Euphrates in western al-Anbar as they struggled to contain insurgent activity from the al-Qaim District to the capital city of ar-Ramadi. Meanwhile, Regimental Combat Team 1 stood poised along Fallujah's outskirts, ready for the likely possibility that the Marines would once again have to enter the city and clear it of insurgent forces. This time it would do so with adequate forces and a well-developed psychological operations plan.

The City and Threat Situation in 2004

The city of Fallujah lies on the Euphrates River at a spot roughly equidistant (about 50 kilometers) from the city of ar-Ramadi and the capital city of Baghdad. The city and its immediate environs occupy an area of about 25 square kilometers, with its northern boundary shaped by a railroad, its west defined by the Euphrates, its east by a highway, and its south by open desert. Highway 10, which crosses the Euphrates to Fallujah's west, divides the city into a northern and southern half. The northern area is dominated by residential areas, with the northwestern Jolan District being the oldest area of the city. Below the Jolan District is the Sook District. The southern area, in particular the city's southeast, is largely industrial. To the east of the industrial sector is a poor residential area that Marines came to call "Queens."

The city is densely populated, and 2003 intelligence estimates indicated its population was between 250,000 and 350,000. The city's 50,000 structures are packed in close

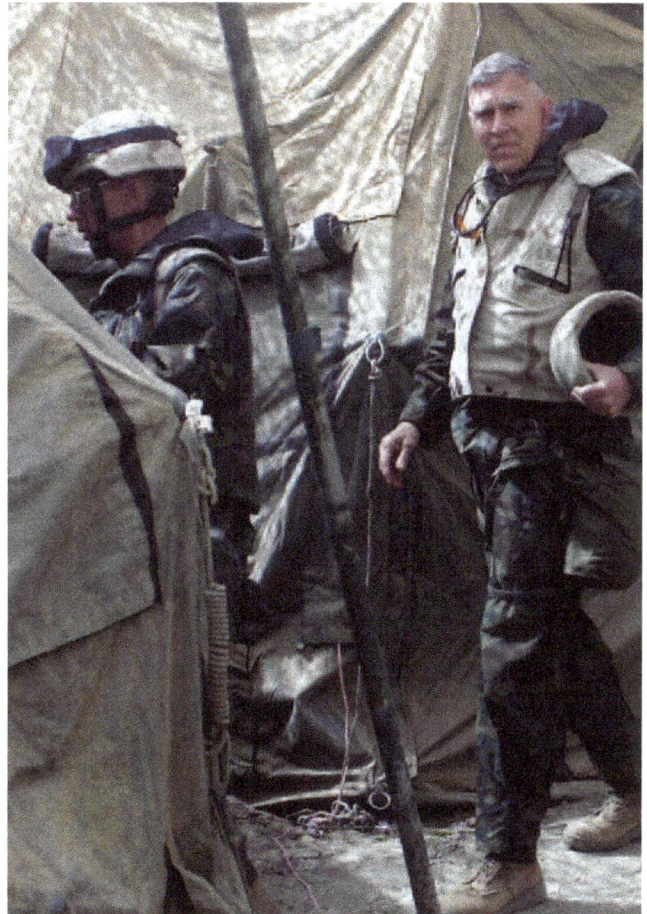

Photo by LCpl Jennifer A. Krusen

Both MajGen James N. Mattis (left), commander of the 1st Marine Division, and LtGen James T. Conway, commander of I Marine Expeditionary Force, cautioned against taking aggressive retaliatory action in Fallujah following the Blackwater killings. Their opposition was ultimately overruled, however.

together, the streets are narrow, and many are lined with walls. This consequently made it difficult for U.S. forces to maneuver vehicles, armored or otherwise, through the city. The minarets of nearly 50 mosques dominate the city skyline, and the city is colloquially known as the "City of Mosques" or the "City of a Hundred Mosques" (there are even more in the outlying neighborhoods and villages).[7]

To the city's west, the Euphrates River takes a sharp bend north then south, creating a peninsula. On the northern tip of this peninsula is a hospital that had been used as an important insurgent information center during the First Battle of Fallujah. Two bridges connect Fallujah to this peninsula. The northern one, the King Faisal Bridge or Old Bridge, is the one on which insurgents had hung the bodies of the murdered Blackwater contractors on 31 March 2004. It is known to Coalition forces by the nickname "Brooklyn Bridge." The southern bridge, called the New Bridge, is the span along which Highway 10 traverses the Euphrates. The northern road crossing the King Faisal

Bridge merges with Highway 10 roughly in the center of the city at the government center. Before they merge, the two roads form two sides of a triangle, with the third side formed by the Euphrates. This triangular section is the al-Andalas District and was nicknamed the "Pizza Slice" by Coalition forces. To the city's east is Highway 1, which runs north south and bisects Highway 10. This intersection is served by a cloverleaf-style interchange.

While many Baath Party officials traced their origins to Fallujah, it would be a mischaracterization to state that opposition to the Coalition in the city stemmed from former regime loyalists. Throughout the 1990s, the city became a center for Salafist Islamic sects, and Saddam often found it difficult to exert his authority over it. For example, during this period Islamic militants destroyed symbols of secular society in the city such as music stores and movie theaters. The city was also dominated by the Dulaim Tribe, another source of opposition to the Coalition. As they had throughout al-Anbar's major urban centers, tribal sheikhs used traditional dominance of old smuggling routes between Syria and Baghdad to grant favors and patronage and build their own authority. The U.S. occupation had hindered these activities, undermining traditional forms of local authority. The Coalition Provisional Authority's decision to abolish the Iraqi army also rendered a significant portion of Fallujah's male populace unemployed, a critical blow to both their means of making a living and their own honor. The order also damaged the city's economy.[8]

Thus the uprising in Fallujah mirrored the general insurgency taking place throughout Iraq: it was a multifaceted movement assembled from former-Baathists, Sunni nationalists, out-of-work veterans, and international Islamist organizations affiliated with al-Qaeda and dedicated to establishing a new fundamentalist state in Iraq. By the time of the two battles for Fallujah, the insurgency had begun to coalesce into a more radical movement with al-Qaeda operative Abu Musab al-Zarqawi emerging as a charismatic and influential leader. In general, the insurgency was united largely only by the shared desire of its members to end the U.S. occupation of the country. Many nationalists and militias aligned with the tribes and found themselves forced into an uneasy alliance with the Islamist organizations led by al-Zarqawi.[9]

Throughout the summer of 2004, Fallujah became an important center for the anti-Coalition insurgency, and al-Zarqawi used it as a base of operations. From the city, he launched terror operations against Baghdad and also carried out high-profile executions against foreigners such as American businessman Nicholas Berg on 7 May

and South Korean missionary Kim Sun-Il on 22 June. Al-Zarqawi's agents assassinated government employees and bombed marketplaces, government buildings, police stations, and international aid stations to coerce the population and make both democracy and cooperation with the United States unworkable. His agents murdered Shia and bombed Shiite mosques with the goal of initiating a civil war and disrupting the transfer of authority from Bremer's Coalition Provisional Authority to the Iraqi Interim Parliament.[10]

The Fallujah Brigade's ineffectiveness allowed insurgents to regroup, consolidate power, and reconstitute with new foreign fighters. Although Fallujah's insurgent groups remained fractured, Abu Musab al-Zarqawi's foreign jihadists and other Islamist groups under Abdullah Janabi and Omar Hadid emerged as the leading insurgent groups in Fallujah. As these groups asserted control over the population, they began enforcing strict Islamic law. They imposed curfews, forced women to cover, and banned Western-style haircuts or Western-style dress. They closed the pool and places where Iraqis could get alcohol or pornography. To get the unwilling population to comply, the jihadists carried out campaigns of intimidation; patrolled the streets to force everyone to conform to their strict Islamic code; and executed men, women, and children for working with the Coalition. In July, insurgent leaders replaced Fallujah's mayor and council with the High Council of Fallujah. The Islamification of Fallujah also kept residents from receiving millions in humanitarian assistance and reconstruction money, which exacerbated the problems afflicting the city.[11]

Insurgent terrorism inside Fallujah peaked during the fall when al-Zarqawi beheaded three British contractors—Eugene Armstrong, Jack Hensley, and Kenneth Bigley—and one Japanese contractor—Shosei Koda—and released videos of the beheadings. Outside Fallujah, insurgent intimidation and violence increased. In July, insurgents kidnapped provincial governor Abdul Karim Burghis al-Rawi's three sons and burned his residence, forcing him to not only resign, but also make an anti-American video.[12]

Thus, by the end of the summer of 2004, it had become clear to both the Coalition commanders and the Iraqi government that a committed, large-scale clearing operation needed to be carried out against the insurgent forces residing in Fallujah. The task for carrying out this operation would fall to the I Marine Expeditionary Force, now commanded by Lieutenant General John F. Sattler, who relieved Lieutenant General Conway on 12 September 2004. Sattler had graduated from the U.S. Naval Academy

LtGen John F. Sattler, commanding general of I Marine Expeditionary Force, was the overall commander of Operation al-Fajr.

in 1971. His distinguished career before assuming command of I MEF included billets as commander of the 2d Marines, assistant division commander of the 2d Marine Division, and director of the Public Affairs Division at Headquarters Marine Corps. Between 2002 and 2004, he served in important commands responsible for fighting the Global War on Terrorism: as commander of the Combined Joint Task Force-Horn of Africa from November 2002 to August 2003 and then as director of operations for U.S. Central Command from August 2003 until 12 September 2004.[13]

Subordinate to Sattler was the new commanding general of the 1st Marine Division, Major General Richard F. Natonski, and the commanding general of the 3d Marine Aircraft Wing, Keith J. Stalder. Major General Natonski was already an Iraq War combat veteran when Major General Mattis transferred command of 1st Marine Division to him on 29 August 2004. During the United States' drive to Baghdad of 2003, he commanded Task Force Tarawa. During the advance, Natonski gained valuable experience leading Marines against irregular forces during the Battle of an-Nasiriyah.[14] Prior to his service in

Iraq, Natonski had served as the commander of the 24th Marine Expeditionary Unit and also occupied important staff billets with Headquarters Marine Corps. Major General Stalder, commander of I MEF's aviation combat element, also had ample command experience during the Global War on Terrorism, having commanded two Marine squadrons in Afghanistan.

In September 2004, as they awaited a decision on when the battle to retake the city would commence, I MEF initiated preliminary operations designed to prepare the battlefield, designated Phase I or "shaping" operations. These had begun in a limited form over the preceding summer. They entailed gathering and staging ammunition, fuel, and other supplies; assembling the combat forces needed for the final assault; and conducting covert and bombing operations to erode the enemy's defenses and their command and control functions. Marines also launched a series of feints and raids intended to test the enemy's capabilities, identify their command and control nodes, gather intelligence, and deceive the enemy of the Coalition's intentions. Ultimately, I MEF hoped to divert the insurgents' attention away from the north (where the as-

November - December 2004

sault force would likely begin its march) toward the south. To strengthen the deception, Marines launched a series of psychological operations, including using loudspeakers to play the sounds of American tanks on the move and fool the insurgents into believing heavy armored forces were amassing along the city's periphery.[15]

As these operations progressed, Marines noticed the insurgents no longer attacked in small groups of 6 to 12 people like they had in April, but were now attempting tactics using larger forces. Marines also witnessed that a precision air strike on insurgent fortifications set off not only a series of explosions from a daisy-chained improvised explosive device (IED) along a primary road but also a series of explosions in the adjoining streets as well. Covert operations gained actionable intelligence on the ground as unmanned aerial vehicles monitored the city 24 hours a day, often catching guerrillas as they reinforced fighting positions, set mines and IEDs, or loaded weapons into cars, homes, and mosques for the impending battle.

I Marine Expeditionary Force also worked to reduce support for the insurgency and create a fissure between the insurgents and the residents of Fallujah.[16] Colonel Robert M. Oliver, information operations officer for I MEF, developed a comprehensive campaign that included radio broadcasts and dropping leaflets on the city with messages designed to drive a wedge between the local citizens and the insurgents. To defeat al-Qaeda's claims that the Coalition's precision attacks against high-value targets only killed innocent noncombatants, these communications told the public who the attacks targeted and why. Colonel Jenny M. Holbert, I MEF's public affairs officer, also brought Western journalists to observe I MEF's planning and operations. Public affairs also conducted an information campaign designed to split the insurgents from the rest of Fallujah's residents by arguing that the insurgents' presence and activities kept locals from receiving humanitarian aid, halted the restoration of essential services, and stalled investment that would revitalize the city. Moreover, these communications also carried Prime Minister Allawi's message to the people of Fallujah stating that if the citizens did not restore order and expel the radical elements on their own, the Iraqi government would support military action.[17]

The Marines hoped to maintain the information initiative by ensuring that plenty of embedded reporters would be on hand to cover the fight once the assault on the city began. Believing the Western media would get the truth on the battle, Colonel Holbert embedded over 90 Western journalists with the assault force. Their only restrictions were that they could not release operational information

that would jeopardize lives, and that if they left their embedded unit, they could not return during the battle.[18]

A final part of the shaping phase called for establishing a sound logistical base for the assault force. To overcome the threat of insurgents attacking supply convoys with improvised explosives and small arms, I Marine Expeditionary Force tasked the 1st Force Service Support Group to build an "iron mountain" of 15 days' worth of food, ammunition, spare parts, and fuel on board each forward operating base prior to commencement of combat operations.[19]

Planning Operation Phantom Fury

By the end of October, the cumulative effects of the preliminary shaping operations had convinced the majority of Fallujah's population to leave the city.[20] The Marines believed there were fewer than 500 civilians remaining in the city alongside 3,000 to 4,500 insurgents. Intelligence calculated that another 1,000 or so insurgents were operating in the entire Fallujah-Ramadi corridor. Coalition intelligence also concluded that "33 of 72 mosques" were "used by insurgents to conduct meetings, store weapons and ammunition, interrogate and torture kidnap victims, and conduct illegal Sharia court sessions."[21] The precision targeting of insurgent safe houses also created tensions among the insurgent groups operating in the city, as some groups believed that the only way the United States could carry out such attacks was if they were receiving intelligence from other insurgent units. In some cases this was certainly true.

Intelligence identified more than 300 well-constructed defensive positions, suggesting that many may have been interlaced with IEDs, a large number of roadblocks, berms, indirect fire positions, sniper and fighting positions, and even daisy-chained IEDs along the city streets. The placement of these defensive positions indicated that I MEF's preliminary attacks and psychological operations had convinced the insurgents that the attack would come from the area around the cloverleaf interchange between Highway 10 and Highway 1 to Fallujah's east, and from the southeast.[22] Marines observed a well-planned "three-ring defense" inside the city as secondary positions along Highway 10 and strongholds in the Jolan District, the Sook District (south of the Jolan), and the Muallimeen District (east of the Sook) showed an insurgent willingness to fight in depth. Captain Jeffrey S. McCormack, operations officer for 3d Battalion, 1st Marines, recalled,

> Basically, the outer ring was going to be what we like to call the cannon fodder. The guys who are the least trained and they'd just throw those guys

Photo by Cpl Daniel J. Fosco

MajGen Richard F. Natonski speaks to Marines in September 2004. Natonski's 1st Marine Division serve as the principal ground headquarters for Operation al-Fajr.

on the periphery of the city to basically be speed bumps for us. As you moved closer into the city you got into more centric ring, more correlated defense, and we knew down south that since April, the last defense, that area of the Nazal, the Shihadi District[s] had been empty of civilians. We'd gotten from multiple sources, we'd confirmed multiple times from [intelligence, surveillance, and reconnaissance] that there was reduced civilian traffic and [we] never saw children down there. The families had basically been kicked out of the area, and that area had become the foreign fighter neighborhood.[23]

With insurgents expecting attacks from the east or south, General Natonski concluded that a southward advance from the north would be the best approach. Once the city's southern approaches were secure with blocking forces, Coalition units would move rapidly from the north through the city clearing houses and other buildings of insurgent forces. The division would also send a light armored task force up the city's western peninsula to insure insurgents could not escape across the Euphrates River. Once the assault force reached the southern boundary of the city, it would then backtrack and continue to clear out residual insurgent forces still occupying the city. The operation would involve not just American forces, but also allied troops from Britain and Iraq.

One of the problems Marines encountered during the April battle for Fallujah was that the slow-moving nature of the attack had given the insurgent forces time to use the mass media to conduct an effective psychological operations campaign. Consequently, Natonski wanted a fast, penetrating attack that would rapidly secure Fallujah with minimal collateral damage and outpace any enemy propaganda efforts. A quick assault would also free up forces in case there were uprisings throughout the remainder of al-Anbar.[24]

General Natonski needed enough units to not only clear the city, but seal it and prevent insurgents from fleeing in the face of the Coalition advance. To address this need, the commander of the Multi-National Corps-Iraq (the command responsible for day-to-day operations throughout Iraq), Lieutenant General Thomas P. Metz III, USA, transferred two Army armored battalions and an Army armored brigade to reinforce the 1st Marine Division. The division's northern assault force would be divided into two regimental combat teams. Regimental Combat Team 1 (formed around the 1st Marines), commanded by Colonel Michael A. Shupp, would include the 3d Battalion, 5th Marines, under Lieutenant Colonel Patrick J. Malay; 3d Battalion, 1st Marines, commanded by Lieutenant Colonel Willard A. Buhl; and the U.S. Army Task Force 2-7 (2d Battalion, 7th Cavalry). Regimental Combat Team 7 (formed around the 7th Marines) was commanded by Colonel Craig A. Tucker and included 1st Battalion, 8th Marines, commanded by Lieutenant Colonel Gareth F. Brandl; 1st Battalion, 3d Marines, commanded by Lieutenant Colonel Michael R. Ramos; and U.S. Army Task Force 2-2 (2d Battalion, 2d Infantry) under Lieutenant Colonel Peter A. Newell, USA.

The 2d Brigade Combat Team (2d Brigade, 1st Cavalry Division), commanded by Colonel Michael D. Formica, would serve as the principal blocking force stationed to Fallujah's south. General Natonski also incorporated elements of the 11th Marine Expeditionary Unit, under Colonel Anthony M. Haslam; the 24th Marine Expeditionary Unit, commanded by Colonel Robert J. Johnson; and the 31st Marine Expeditionary Unit, commanded by Colonel Walter L. Miller Jr. Essential to the battle was the

The city of Fallujah in November 2004. This image presents many of the city's defining characteristics: its tightly packed buildings, narrow streets, and numerous mosques.

inclusion of Iraqi security forces. These forces had to be brought into Fallujah from outside al-Anbar Province because Anbari soldiers would not fight their own tribesmen or other regional tribes. All in all, the attack force included nine U.S. Army and Marine battalions and six Iraqi battalions (12,000 Marines, soldiers, sailors, airmen, and Iraqi security forces). For the battle, I Marine Expeditionary Force would grow from 32,000 to 45,000 personnel.[25]

Phantom Fury's planners placed a grid of imaginary phase lines onto Fallujah to coordinate maneuvers. Most of these ran along the city's major thoroughfares. Phase lines running north to south were designated with male code names, while phase lines moving west to east were given female code names. Running along Fallujah's northern boundary was Alternate Supply Route Golden. Running west to east through the Jolan District was Phase Line Cathy. Phase Line Elizabeth ran from the peninsula across the King Faisal Bridge, through the city to the cloverleaf. Phase Line Fran ran from the peninsula, across the Euphrates and ended at the government center. Phase Line Isabel ran from the east bank of the Euphrates to

"Queens" District while Phase Line Jenna ran across the city's southern border.

Running from north to south were Phase Lines Henry, Ethan, and Dave. Phase Line Henry emanated from Alternate Supply Route Golden and proceeded south through the Jolan District, the "pizza slice," and to the southern edges of the city. East of Phase Line Henry, Phase Line Ethan moved south past Highway 10 and then proceeded along the boundary between "Queens" and the industrial sector, ending at the south. To the east of Ethan was Phase Line Dave, which ran from Route Golden to Highway 10.

Decisive operations to secure Fallujah would begin when Regimental Combat Teams 1 and 7 breached the railroad tracks running along Fallujah's northern perimeter that separated the 1st Marine Division's assault force from the city. Once the two regiments traversed the tracks, they would push rapidly into Fallujah to Highway 10 (Phase Line Fran). As the division's main effort, Regimental Combat Team 1 would attack rapidly down the western section along the Euphrates River and seize the

Battle for Fallujah

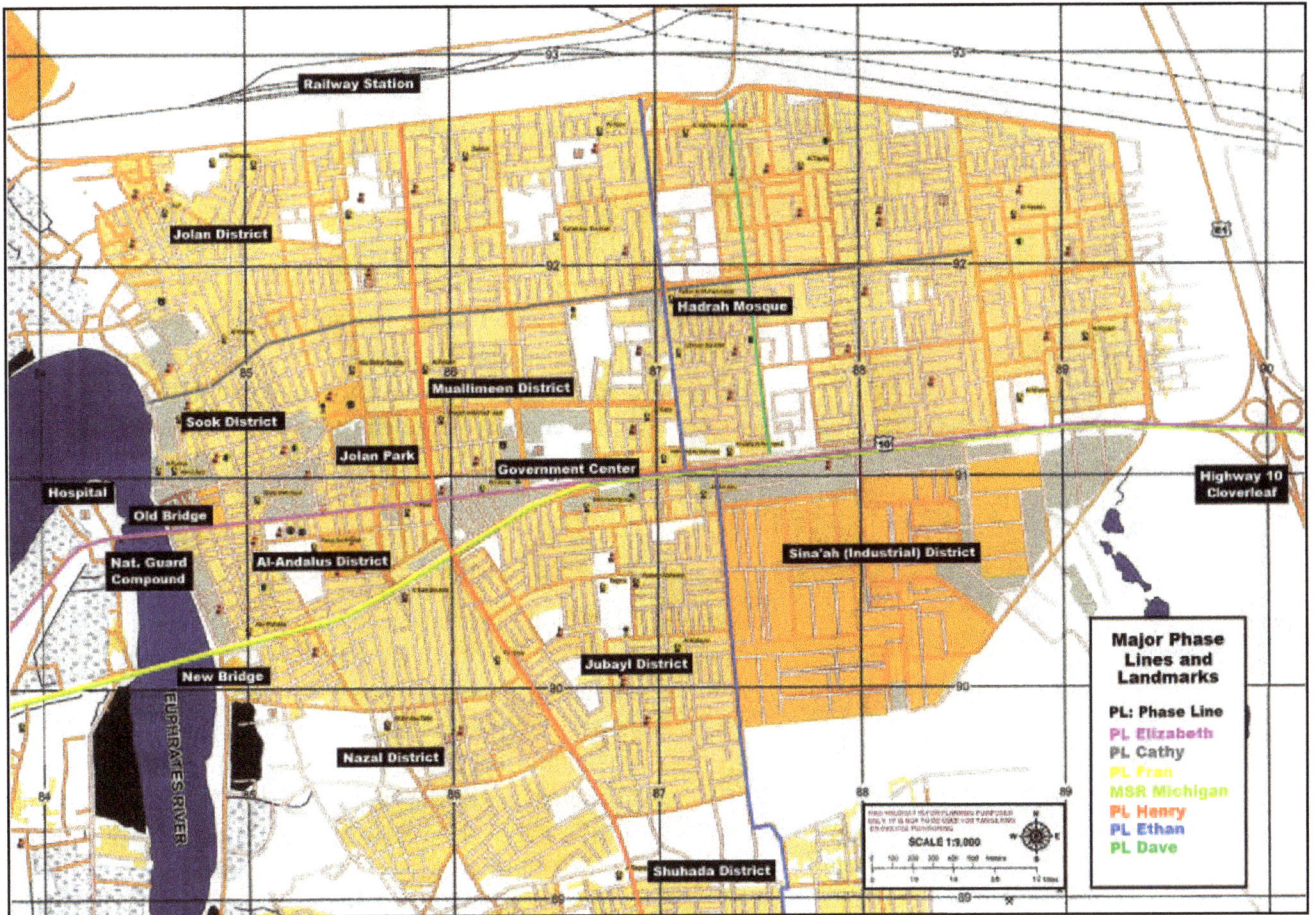

Map of Fallujah with major phase lines and landmarks.

most crucial position in the city, the Jolan District, which included Jolan Park. This district was not only the oldest and the most populated of the city but was also Fallujah's spiritual base. Furthermore, it was thought to hold the enemy's main command and control node.

The plan to seize and secure the Jolan called for the 3d Battalion, 5th Marines, to plunge into the district and attack the insurgent forces head on. Regimental Combat Team 1's remaining two battalions would then sweep, south by west, toward the Euphrates River, pinning the insurgent forces between the 3d Battalion, 5th Marines, and the 3d Battalion, 1st Marines. The assault battalions would either kill the insurgents in place or push them toward the river.[26]

Meanwhile, Task Force 2-7 would push quickly south along Phase Line Henry on the edge of the Jolan District, destroying insurgent defenses and cohesion. After securing Jolan Park, Task Force 2-7 would continue attacking south along Phase Line Henry to Phase Line Fran, then turn west to secure a school located in the "pizza slice." The 3d Battalion, 1st Marines, would attack and destroy insurgents behind Task Force 2-7, clearing buildings as it

established a line of communication for resupply and evacuations along Phase Line Henry. Iraqi soldiers would help search and clear buildings or areas not cleared in the initial assault. Task Force 2-7 would then finish securing Main Supply Route Michigan between Phase Line Henry and the two Euphrates River crossings, and 3d Battalion, 1st Marines, would continue west and attack to secure the al-Kabir Mosque.[27]

Meanwhile, Regimental Combat Team 7 would advance through the eastern half of Fallujah to Phase Line Fran. Its three assault battalions would then turn toward the Euphrates River. Because of its speed and mobility, Task Force 2-2's armor would lead the way, pushing through the city on the regimental combat team's eastern flank to secure Main Supply Route Michigan. This was a crucial mission for Task Force 2-2 because the highway was going to be the main supply route from Camp Fallujah to combat forces in the city. At the same time, 1st Battalion, 3d Marines, and 1st Battalion, 8th Marines, would advance with Task Force 2-2 to Phase Line Fran, but not as quickly. The 1st Battalion, 8th Marines, would attack on the western flank down Phase Line Ethan and 3d Bat-

Photo by Sgt Paul L. Anstine II

Col Craig A. Tucker, commanding officer of Regimental Combat Team 7, speaks to Marines and soldiers in Iraq in March 2004.

talion, 1st Marines, along Phase Line Dave.[28] At that point, the two Marine battalions would turn west toward the Euphrates River, moving behind Task Force 2-2, and drive Fallujah's remaining insurgents into the water. The entire plan centered on rapid penetration into the city, using the shock, firepower, and mobility of the U.S. Army's heavy armor of Task Force 2-7 and Task Force 2-2 to overwhelm Fallujah's insurgents.

Intelligence reports received during the period before the battle seemed to indicate that the insurgents in Fallujah were planning to leave the city to attack targets throughout al-Anbar Province, including major supply routes and other cities. However, meeting the force requirements for the Fallujah assault force necessitated moving Regimental Combat Team 7 from its positions in western al-Anbar, potentially threatening the security in that region as well as al-Anbar's capital city, ar-Ramadi.[29] Natonski subsequently redeployed and reinforced his units throughout his area of responsibility. In ar-Ramadi, he augmented the U.S. Army 2d Brigade Combat Team, 2d Infantry Division, commanded by Colonel Gary S.

Patton, USA, to counter potential insurgent activity there during the battle.[30] Natonski also tasked the British Black Watch Battalion; the 2d Battalion, 24th Marines; and the 24th Marine Expeditionary Unit with securing the insurgents' lines of communication between Fallujah and Babil Province to the southeast.[31]

The 3d Marine Aircraft Wing would provide support in the form of fixed-wing McDonnell Douglas F/A-18D Hornet fighter attack jets and McDonnell Douglas AV-8B Harrier attack planes. Rotary-wing assets included the venerable Bell UH-1Y Venom and Bell AH-1W Cobra attack helicopters, Boeing Vertol CH-46 Sea Knight medium helicopters, and Sikorsky CH-53E Super Stallions. The Army, Navy, and Air Force also provided aviation assets, including the formidable U.S. Air Force Lockheed AC-130H Spectre gunships.

Division planners faced an important challenge in regard to aviation, which was how to coordinate the large number of Coalition aircraft expected to provide close air support in the small target area of Fallujah. The high volume of indirect fire and unmanned aerial vehicles posed other challenges. Marine air planners developed a system called "keyhole," which involved vertically separating the different types of aircraft and projectiles over a five-mile circle over Fallujah and ar-Ramadi. Rotary-wing attack aircraft would operate on the city's fringes below 1,500 feet. They would not be allowed over the city, but would rather be posted at battle positions outside the city's boundaries and be available when specifically requested. Fixed-wing aircraft would stay above 9,000 feet and would not be allowed within the five-mile circle unless they were cleared by a regimental or battalion air officer—or were talking to a forward air controller—and were ready to immediately attack a target. Artillery, mortar fires, and a dense assortment of unmanned aerial vehicles would operate in between. Until they were cleared into the keyhole, fixed-wing aircraft were stacked at points north, east, south, and west, around Fallujah, outside the five-mile keyhole but within a 15-mile outer perimeter. They would be available at a moment's notice.

Only one aircraft would be allowed directly over the city at a time. Once in the keyhole, fixed-wing aircraft had free reign to maneuver in order to maximize their chances of hitting the assigned targets. However, they had to get ordnance on target quickly because other forward air controllers were waiting their turns. The helicopters, like artillery, would be employed at any time in a battalion's zone with no coordination beyond that of the battalion's forward air controller. Management of fixed-wing close air support was almost as easy, only requiring coor-

Battle for Fallujah

Photo by LCpl William L. Dubose III

The 3d Marine Aircraft Wing, commanded by MajGen Keith J. Stalder (fourth from left), was responsible for coordinating and conducting air operations throughout the operation to clear Fallujah.

dination between the direct air support center and the two regiments. With their plan approved by Multi-National Force-Iraq and Multi-National Corps-Iraq, the Marines took control of air operations over Fallujah from the U.S. Air Force for the battle. This not only gave Marines the unity of command and control they hoped would foster efficiency and speed while minimizing fratricide, but also allowed the U.S. Air Force to concentrate on operations outside Fallujah.[32]

Part of the planning for the battle included the creation of a robust civil affairs program for the postbattle period. Many weeks prior to the battle, Regimental Combat Team 1's Civil Affairs Detachment 4-4 met with a group of Fallujans called the Fallujah Liaison Team at the civil-military operations center outside the city to gain their cooperation in rebuilding Fallujah after the battle. These municipal workers, police officers, businessmen, doctors, and technocrats provided useful information to civil affairs personnel about the location and condition of the city's infrastructure, such as the hospitals, water plants, and the electrical grid. The Marines also used this infor-

mation to place restricted fire areas on key infrastructure to protect them from collateral damage.

During their planning, civil affairs detachment teams "war gamed" postbattle operations to anticipate what damage would occur in order to prioritize critical reconstruction projects. Planners divided the postbattle operations into three phases: civil affairs (reconstruction and humanitarian aid), repopulating the city, and conducting the national elections on 30 January 2005. The 4th Civil Affairs Group was in direct support of the 1st Marine Division during the assault on the city, with Civil Affairs Detachment 4-4, supporting Regimental Combat Team 1 and U.S. Army Company B, 445th Civil Affairs Battalion, supporting Regimental Combat Team 7.[33]

Throughout the preparation and shaping phase, General Sattler met with General George W. Casey, USA, commander of the Multi-National Force-Iraq, the overall headquarters for Coalition forces in Iraq. In late October, Generals Sattler, Casey, and Metz finally met with Prime Minister Allawi and presented him with their plan. They also provided the prime minister with video footage of precision bombing strikes that convinced him that Fallujah's streets were deserted and that the Marines would not level the city.[34] Lieutenant General Sattler asked for assurance from the prime minister that he would not suspend the assault once it had begun. "I looked him right in the eye," Lieutenant General Sattler recalled, and said,

> You know, Mr. Prime Minister, don't tell us to go and expect us to stop. When you have exhausted all the political, all the opportunities to solve this problem, and that we can no longer let them export their terrorist ideas, their VBIEDs [vehicle-borne improvised explosive devices], their IEDs [improvised explosive devices], their raids. . . . When you reach that point, I actually said, just tear your phone out of the wall. Don't think about calling us and telling us to stop because once we get going, we're going to have to go all the way. We're not gonna stop 'til we hit the southern end of the town. . . . And, he said, I understand. When I tell you go, we will accomplish the mission, we will complete the mission.[35]

During the meeting, Prime Minister Allawi requested that the name of the operation be changed from Phantom Fury to al-Fajr, Arabic for "New Dawn," so that Iraqis would be able to identify with and better understand the coming battle.[36] In a video conference several days prior to the attack, President Bush gave General Casey the green light for the attack and assured him that once the attack began it would not be halted.[37]

During October, Major General Natonski moved his forward headquarters from Camp Blue Diamond in ar-Ramadi to Camp Fallujah. Brigadier General Joseph F. Dunford Jr., the assistant division commander, remained at Camp Blue Diamond and oversaw the rest of al-Anbar Province.[38] In late October, units of the Fallujah assault force began to arrive. Marine reconnaissance and U.S. Navy Sea, Air, Land (SEAL) teams assigned to both Regimental Combat Teams 1 and 7 began operations on Fallujah's periphery in preparation for the impending battle. Their missions included searching the area in northern Fallujah where the regiment's forces were to enter the city, primarily checking for improvised explosive devices and locations of insurgent observation posts.[39]

In western al-Anbar, the 31st Marine Expeditionary Unit, taking control from Regimental Combat Team 7, began conducting helicopter raids over the vast area of operation and used Marine heliborne forces to conduct snap vehicle checkpoints on the main supply routes. Meanwhile, the U.S. Army's 2d Brigade Combat Team (2d Brigade, 2d Infantry Division), increased disruption

Photo by LCpl Ryan B. Bussel

A view of Fallujah's abandoned train station, which served as the forward headquarters for Regimental Combat Team 1 during the Second Battle of Fallujah.

operations on the western side of the Euphrates River from Fallujah and the ar-Ramadi area.

Sealing the City

I Marine Expeditionary Force held a confirmation brief on 1 November 2004 during which Generals Sattler and Natonski and their subordinates apprised Generals Casey and Metz of the pending attack.[40] During the five days following the briefing, the two assault regiments conducted in-depth planning and rehearsal-of-concept drills.[41] For most units, this included preparing full operations orders and building terrain models of the city based on detailed maps that numbered blocks and buildings, and labeling phase lines.[42]

Meanwhile, I MEF increased nightly monitoring and targeting of insurgents inside Fallujah, destroying targets once they gained positive identification that insurgents occupied them. They also used U.S. Air Force AC-130 gunships to destroy targets identified as insurgent centers by Marines from the 2d Radio Battalion.

Marines similarly conducted operations to disrupt insurgents operating farther beyond Fallujah's periphery, concentrating on the insurgent supply lines running from southern Fallujah to Baghdad through northern Babil Province. During multiple operations, the 24th Marine Expeditionary Unit, working with Iraqi security forces, captured 41 insurgents on 5 November.[43]

Also, on 5 November, the first elements of the U.S. Army's 2d Brigade Combat Team (2d Brigade, 1st Cavalry Division) moved into positions outside Fallujah. The brigade deployed a mechanized infantry battalion, designated Task Force 1-5 Infantry (1st Battalion, 5th Infantry), and commanded by Lieutenant Colonel Todd McCaffrey, USA, to the south of the city. The task force's orders were to prevent insurgents from leaving the city, conduct offensive operations to disrupt insurgents in the area, and protect the 1st Marine Division's flank during the battle. Once in place, Task Force 1-5 Infantry began conducting cordons and searches to disrupt the enemy.[44] The battalion was equipped with M1A2 Abrams tanks, M2A3 Bradley fighting vehicles, various types of General Dynamics Stryker light armored vehicles, and M1114 up-armored humvees.

The brigade deployed a second battalion, Task Force 1-5 Cavalry (1st Battalion, 5th Cavalry), commanded by Lieutenant Colonel Myles M. Miyamasu, USA, to block the approaches to the city in the northeast. The cavalry battalion's Strykers assumed a position in northeast Fallujah, while the 759th Military Police Battalion maintained security on Highway 1 from Fallujah to Baghdad, and the 6th Battalion, 3d Brigade, Iraqi Army, maintained checkpoints along the highways.[45] The perimeter swept about 270 degrees around Fallujah.[46] The 2d Reconnaissance Battalion—the 1st Marine Division's main blocking force—reinforced with Company A, 2d Light Armored Reconnaissance Battalion; a platoon of M1A1 tanks from the 11th Marine Expeditionary Unit; a mechanized infantry platoon from Company C, 1st Battalion, 5th Cavalry; and Iraqi special forces moved closer to block the southeast of the city, focusing on Phase Line Henry. During the battle, they would conduct several supporting operations in the Fallujah-Ramadi corridor to disrupt insurgent activity.[47] This was a likely possibility, as intelligence reports indicated that many insurgents had left the city to attack Coalition forces on the highways and in other major cities, such as ar-Ramadi and Husaybah, as they had during the first battle. These insurgents included leaders who claimed they would fight to the death.[48]

Supporting Colonel Formica's blocking force were four dedicated aircraft from the U.S. Army's 4th Aviation Brigade, 1st Cavalry Division, which provided continuous aerial reconnaissance and security missions using AH-64D attack helicopters and OH-58D helicopters. The helicopters also destroyed insurgent rocket launchers and insurgent boats used to transport weapons across the Euphrates River. These forces helped isolate Fallujah and reinforced the insurgents' belief that the Coalition would attack from the south. They also convinced large groups of civilians to leave, and the soldiers and Marines sealing

United States Air Force AC-130 gunships, such as the one pictured here, provided critical close air support to the Marines and soldiers advancing through the city of Fallujah in November 2004.

the city would allow numerous groups of civilians fleeing on foot to escape, except military-age men 16 to 55. Later that day, they would cover the movement of the remaining division forces as they moved into their staging positions north of the city.[49]

Meanwhile, as Colonel Formica's blocking forces moved into position, the first of the division's assault forces were moving into their attack positions. The force conducted a full rehearsal on 6 November. This included attacking enemy positions with air and artillery; executing the movement of attack forces from their assembly areas to their attack positions; testing command, control, and communications; conducting a reconnaissance in force; and making a feint north to deceive the insurgent forces.[50] During this rehearsal, Regimental Combat Team 7's reconnaissance and SEAL teams also entered the city as part of Task Force High Value Target.[51] In Regimental Combat Team 1's attack positions, 3d Battalion, 5th Marines, prepared for the initial assault into the Jolan District. To ensure that it had the necessary combat support assets and personnel, the battalion's executive officer, Major Todd S. Degrosseilliers, assembled a provisional unit from 3d Battalion, 5th Marines' Weapons Company and Headquarters and Service Company and created Task Force Stryker.[52]

On 7 November, a light armored reconnaissance task force commanded by Lieutenant Colonel Stephen R. Dinauer moved from its staging area at Camp Habbaniyah toward its attack positions on the peninsula west of the city, on the other side of the Euphrates. The force, Task Force Wolfpack, was made up of Company C, 3d Light

Soldiers from the 2d Brigade Combat Team (2d Brigade, 1st Cavalry Division) advance into Fallujah on 9 November 2004. The 2d Brigade Combat Team served as a blocking force along Fallujah's western and southern border, trapping insurgents inside the city as the 1st Marine Division's two assault regiments moved southward.

Armored Reconnaissance Battalion; a reinforced infantry company (Company B, 1st Battalion, 23d Marines); and a reinforced mechanized infantry company (the U.S. Army's Company C, 1st Battalion, 9th Infantry).

Also assigned to Task Force Wolfpack was the Small Craft Company from the 2d Marine Division that included five 35-foot riverine assault craft that moved into positions on the river northwest of the peninsula's tip to seal access to the city by water from the north. Task Force Wolfpack's mission was to attack up the peninsula and secure the two key bridges leading into Fallujah from the peninsula to prevent enemy reinforcement or escape from the city. They also sought to secure the hospital on the peninsula's tip to prevent its use as a command center, weapons storage facility, and platform for insurgent propaganda. Finally, the task force was to secure the adjacent 506th Iraqi National Guard compound on the river just below the King Faisal Bridge.[53]

That same day Iraqi radio and television broadcast two messages from the Iraqi interim government. The first

proclaimed the government's intention to reestablish control of Fallujah and to liberate the citizens from the insurgents. The second was the declaration of a "state of emergency" in Iraq. The government banned vehicle traffic in and around Fallujah and imposed a curfew in the Fallujah-Ramadi area. Many Iraqis in al-Anbar, however, opposed Prime Minister Ayad Allawi's declaration. In ar-Ramadi, the police deserted and the Iraqi National Guard was ineffective because of the insurgent fear and intimidation campaign. In other areas around Iraq, insurgents increased their attacks against Coalition forces and the Iraqi interim government.[54]

Opening Maneuvers: Task Force Wolfpack on the Peninsula

At 1900 on 7 November 2004, Marines launched a limited number of precision air strikes on the insurgents' defensive positions, weapons caches, and command and control centers inside the city using a variety of Coalition aircraft. They struck 9 of the approximately 60 preplanned

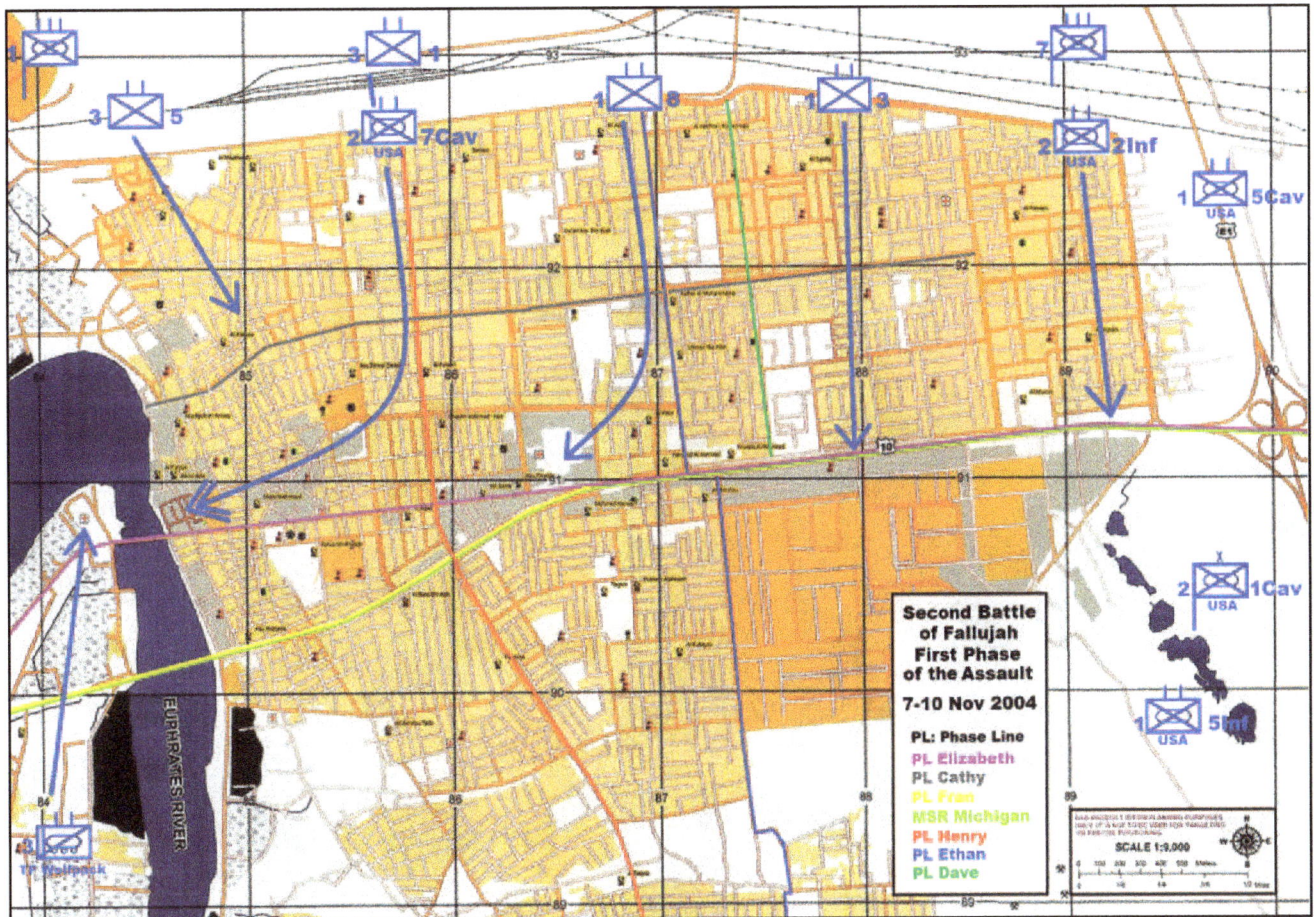

Second Battle
of Fallujah
First Phase
of the Assault
7-10 Nov 2004

PL: Phase Line
PL Elizabeth
PL Cathy
PL Fran
MSR Michigan
PL Henry
PL Ethan
PL Dave

SCALE 1:9,000

Official U.S. Marine Corps map adapted by History Division

targets while additional air strikes eliminated insurgents firing on Coalition forces. The remainder of targets were not hit because of collateral damage concerns. As the U.S. troops moved into their assault positions, the lethal 155mm howitzer fires of Battery M, 4th Battalion, 14th Marines; Battery C, 1st Battalion, 12th Marines; and the self-propelled M109A6 Paladins from the U.S. Army's Battery A, 3d Battalion, 82d Field Artillery provided covering fire. Marines also engaged in electronic attacks that jammed insurgent communications and conducted psychological operations to confuse the enemy and convince remaining noncombatants to leave.[55]

At 1900, as coordinated artillery and air strikes hit Fallujah, Lieutenant Colonel Stephen R. Dinauer's Task Force Wolfpack began its attack up Fallujah's western peninsula. Major Michael Miller Jr.'s Company B, 1st Battalion, 23d Marines, moved up the peninsula's western side along the river and Main Supply Route Michigan, while the Marines of Company C, 3d Light Armored Reconnaissance Battalion under Captain Scott M. Conway moved up the peninsula's eastern side. At the same time, the soldiers, tanks, and Bradleys from Company C, 1st Battalion, 9th Infantry, and a platoon of Marines from

Company B, 1st Battalion, 23d Marines, proceeded up the center of the peninsula toward the two bridges spanning the Euphrates as the 36th Iraqi Commando Battalion moved quickly toward the hospital at the end of the peninsula.

Within five minutes after crossing the line of departure, Captain Conway's light armored vehicle struck an IED, temporarily knocking his driver unconscious. However, the company soon continued attacking east across the peninsula to the western bank of the Euphrates River then headed north toward the bridges. When Conway's company reached the limit of its attack, the Marines established checkpoints and began clearing from north to south, searching houses and establishing support-by-fire locations along the river. As his company cleared the peninsula, Conway and his Marines came under enemy fire and received shrapnel from friendly air and artillery missions attacking preplanned targets across the river.[56]

By 2100, Task Force Wolfpack had secured the western ends of the bridges and Army Sappers attached to the task force began constructing blocking positions and support-by-fire locations. By 2300, Iraqi commandos had seized

Photo by SrA Christopher A. Marasky, USAF

A Marine LAV-25 guards a checkpoint in Fallujah on 15 November 2004. On 7 November 2004, Task Force Wolfpack, equipped with LAVs, seized the hospital and National Guard Headquarters on Fallujah's western peninsula.

the Fallujah hospital with no resistance, and by 0140 on 8 November, Task Force Wolfpack secured all objectives and obstacles on the bridges. Just offshore, Major Daniel J. Wittnam's Small Craft Company drifted around the tip of the peninsula within sight of the King Faisal Bridge and encountered fire from insurgents in the Jolan District.[57]

Throughout the night of 7 November and into the morning of the 8th, the Marines closely monitored Fallujah using unmanned aerial vehicles. Marines watched in real time on the command post's large projection screens as insurgents were destroyed with the use of coordinated air and artillery strikes as they assembled and manned their positions. At the same time, two AC-130H gunships identified and killed insurgents as they circled overhead at 9,000–11,000 feet. During the battle, a gunship would be assigned to each assault regiment. The continuous bombardment was effective in destroying defensive positions and weapons caches and disrupting insurgent command and control abilities. It was also effective in convincing the enemy that this was the main attack.[58]

On Fallujah's northern edge, Task Force High Value Target moved about 300 meters to the northeast to a cluster of three buildings (about 500 meters from the edge of the city) to keep out of the way of the assault force as it came into position and linked up with 1st Battalion, 8th Marines. The night was relatively uneventful as the SEALs and reconnaissance Marines of the task force maintained surveillance on the city. On Fallujah's southern edge, Company B, 2d Reconnaissance Battalion, attacked northward to Fallujah's southern limits to clear the area of insurgents and then established a combat outpost in the highest building in the area from which they observed the southern city. Because of the heavy concentration of insurgent forces, southern Fallujah would remain a kill zone subject to Coalition air and artillery strikes until the soldiers and Marines of the 1st Marine Division assault force attacked into southern Fallujah later in the battle.[59]

After completing communications checks, the 1st Marine Division assault force began tactical movements to its attack positions north of the city. Through the night of 7 November and into the day of 8 November, the two regi-

F/A-18D Hornet fighter-bombers such as the one from Marine All-Weather Fighter Attack Squadron 224 pictured here at al-Asad in 2005, provided valuable close air support during the Second Battle of Fallujah.

ments moved slowly on a makeshift road marked by infrared chemical lights, snaking through the gravel pits, sand quarries, and homes that dotted the terrain north of the city.[60] In all, more than 1,000 vehicles moved through the night. "During the leader's recon," Lieutenant Colonel Michael R. Ramos recalled, "there were 20- to 30-foot deep quarries in the area, and there are narrow land bridges across those quarries, where if you didn't see the drop off on the left and right side, you could easily roll a tank inside there, or collapse one of the land bridges across. There were some swampy areas that you could easily get a [Caterpillar] D9 bulldozer or an amphibious assault vehicle stuck and mired up through the top of the tracks."[61]

By the morning of 8 November, Regimental Combat Teams 1 and 7 had arrived at their final attack positions and almost immediately encountered enemy fire.[62] Once in their attack positions, General Natonski's two reinforced regiments covered the entire length of Fallujah's northern boundary in a near-linear formation with only a few hundred yards of desert separating the massive assault force from the city. The city was completely encir-

cled, the first time that the Coalition had sufficient troops to seal the city.[63]

As the six assault battalions made their final preparations, General Natonski visited each of the units at their attack positions.[64] Waiting for the assault to begin, soldiers and Marines dug fighting positions as cover from indirect fire, others waited in tanks and amphibious assault vehicles amid intermittent rain, and engineers fortified positions along the division's line of departure.[65] Some Marines would wait as long as 20 hours for the assault to begin. "We set in the attack position all day, just listening and watching the bombardment," Captain Jer J. Garcia, commanding officer, Company B, 1st Battalion, 3d Marines, recalled. "Fallujah was just on fire. It was just getting pounded."[66] U.S. Army Major Lisa J. DeWitt, a Task Force 2-2 surgeon, recalled, "It was a really, really big fireworks show. I remember thinking to myself, 'I'll never go to a 4th of July fireworks show with the same thoughts ever again.' "[67]

In northwest Fallujah, Task Force Stryker established the northern blocking position along Alternate Supply

Route Golden. This allowed Company K and Company L of 3d Battalion, 5th Marines, to move south, establish a southern blocking position along the supply route, and begin the assault on Regimental Combat Team 1's first objective, an apartment complex. Soon thereafter, Company K, 3d Battalion, 5th Marines, commanded by Captain Andrew J. McNulty, moved quickly to secure the objective around 1000, with Task Force Stryker's lead elements following directly behind. As it moved its units into position, 3d Battalion, 5th Marines, came under fire from insurgent mortars, rocket-propelled grenades, and small-arms fire emanating from across the railroad tracks.[68]

In the hours before the assault, several of Regimental Combat Team 1's company commanders and key staff made a final reconnaissance of the breach sites with the protection of Task Force 2-7's tanks and Bradley fighting vehicles. Captain Robert J. Bodisch Jr., commanding officer of Company C, 2d Tank Battalion, made two reconnaissance trips to the Fallujah train station, each time coming under insurgent fire. Bodisch provided six Abrams tanks to 3d Battalion, 5th Marines, and eight tanks to 3d Battalion, 1st Marines.[69]

Insurgents had mined the railroad overpass bridge south of the apartment complex and much of the land south of the railroad was deeply pitted and covered with debris. This presented the 3d Battalion, 5th Marines, with a significant challenge getting into the city. To resolve this dilemma, battalion commander Lieutenant Colonel Malay decided to breach the tracks with an airstrike west of the overpass bridge, where the tracks rested upon a 30-meter-high earthen berm. At around 1400, four F/A-18Ds of Marine All-Weather Fighter Attack Squadron 242 dropped eight laser-guided, 2,000-pound GBU-31 bombs on the tracks. The mission was led by Major General Stalder.

Meanwhile, about a kilometer east along the railroad tracks from the apartment complex, elements of 3d Battalion, 1st Marines, had been exchanging fire with insurgents across the railroad tracks since coming into their attack positions. There had been no preassault fires here, and insurgents occupied homes and defensive positions along the road that paralleled the railroad tracks and Alternate Supply Route Golden. From their attack positions north of Fallujah's railway station, 3d Battalion, 1st Marines, prepared for its assault on the station while the soldiers of Task Force 2-7 prepared to lead the way across the breach as soon as 3d Battalion, 1st Marines, and Iraqi forces secured their objective.[70]

Further east, in Regimental Combat Team 7's sector, Colonel Craig A. Tucker and his battalion and company commanders walked out from their attack positions to the line of departure, just off the railroad tracks, to identify the best routes into the city.[71] "The terrain sucked," observed Lieutenant Colonel Newell, commanding officer of Task Force 2-2. "It was hard to move around in and hard to find a place to penetrate, and then you had that railroad track embankment," which posed a problem for the force's wheeled vehicles.[72] Soon thereafter, at about 0940, Lieutenant Colonel Newell positioned his brigade reconnaissance troop in the northeast sector of the city that looked down on enemy positions. "We actually started moving in the daylight about early afternoon," Newell recalled. "The plan was to set the brigade recon troop up in the northeast corner, on the high ground overlooking the city, so he could look down into the daylight into where the breach area was and the two blocks to the south. The bottom line is that I wanted him to shoot anything that moved in that area."

During the day, U.S. Army Captain Kirk A. Mayfield's brigade reconnaissance troop engaged targets within two blocks of the breach with snipers, mortars, and artillery to force insurgents to leave positions across from the breach. However, with the advantage of a long-range advanced scout surveillance system, Mayfield's soldiers also attacked targets deep into Task Force 2-2 battlespace, fracturing enemy cohesion. "They're driving up and down looking at the crossroads behind the blocks," said Newell, "Essentially they were ambushing guys . . . [and] were very effective in cleaning the area out for several hours."[73]

On the western peninsula, Task Force Wolfpack's executive officer, Major Kenneth R. Kassner, escorted a civil affairs group assessment team to Fallujah hospital where they surveyed the hospital and unloaded medical and humanitarian assistance supplies. Soldiers from the Iraqi interim forces raised the Iraqi flag at the hospital, which drew a large volume of small-arms and indirect fire from Fallujah's insurgents in the Jolan District throughout the day of 8 November. East of Fallujah, soldiers and Marines began to see more activity by insurgents attacking forces with IEDs, indirect fire, and small-arms ambushes. Insurgents hit one of Task Force Wolfpack's ammo resupply convoys on Alternate Supply Route Boston with indirect fire, which destroyed a seven-ton truck and caused multiple casualties. Another Task Force Wolfpack convoy struck an IED that killed two Marines from Combat Service Support Company 113 and wounded another. Insurgents on Fallujah's periphery also fired on U.S. Army helicopters. In southern Fallujah, soldiers and Marines began to see an increase in the numbers of civilians attempting to leave.[74]

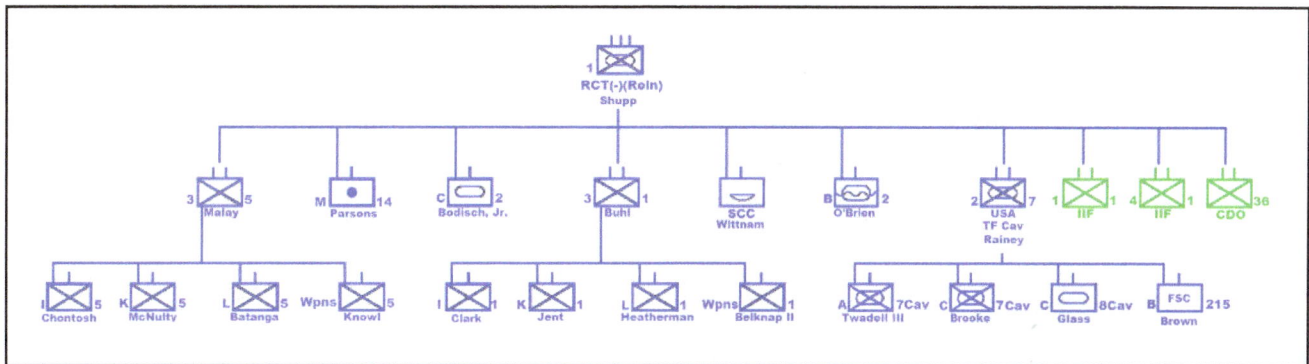

Diagram of Regimental Combat Team 1 during Operation al-Fajr.

8 November:
The Assault into the Jolan District

As dusk approached on the evening of 8 November, after many long hours of anticipation, Major General Richard Natonski's six assault battalions prepared to advance. Finally, as nighttime fell over the city, Navy construction battalions ("Seabees") and Marines from the 4th Civil Affairs Group, in direct support of the 1st Marine Division, entered the electricity substation just west of the apartment complex and cut Fallujah's power supply. Only those residents and insurgents with their own generators would have power for such things as charging their cell phones. At the same time, Company L, 3d Battalion, 1st Marines, and Company D, Iraqi National Guard, crept closer to Fallujah's train station in preparation for their attack. Then, at 1900, under the cover of darkness and amid pouring rain, the 1st Marine Division began its assault of Fallujah.

In Regimental Combat Team 1's sector, Company L, 3d Battalion, 1st Marines, moved to take on the train station by firing tank rounds into the building and bracketing it with indirect fire to disrupt insurgents who fired small arms and rocket-propelled grenades. Iraqi National Guard soldiers attached to Company L then went into the building as Marines and a tank section provided support. The station was secured by 2034. With the train station secure, 3d Battalion, 1st Marines, assembled in serialized order under enemy fire behind the U.S. Army tanks of Task Force 2-7 as engineers worked to breach the four sets of railroad tracks on the steep earthen berm and cut a path through the mines.[75] U.S. Marine tanks from Company C, 2d Tank Battalion, then established a support-by-fire location near the tracks where they engaged insurgents and destroyed barriers and suspected car bombs.[76]

At 1926, 3d Battalion, 5th Marines, launched its assault into the Jolan District, following the battalion's two main tanks through a cut in the berm west of the train station.

Company K, 3d Battalion, 5th Marines, provided support-by-fire from the apartment complex while Company I passed through the breach in amphibious tracked vehicles behind a section of Marine tanks from Company C, 2d Tank Battalion. Company L, similarly equipped, attacked along the river toward the palm grove. After dismounting, Company I overwhelmed insurgents fighting from the Jolan cemetery and then seized the Ma'ahidy Mosque.[77]

Watching from the roof of the apartment complex, Regimental Combat Team 1 commanding officer, Colonel Michael A. Shupp, observed,

> Third Battalion, 5th Marines, was making such incredible progress it was unbelievable. They were just blowing through that push. And it completely unhinged the enemy, because they were coming behind their defenses, behind the cemetery on the north side of the city, where they had all sorts of firing holes and positions against the cemetery wall north of the northern approach.[78]

Unfortunately, the breach at the train station did not go as smoothly. Despite damage to the railroad track and berms, the M58 rocket-propelled mine-clearing line charges failed to provide adequate breaching lanes for the Marines to pass through. Engineers cut the tracks with TNT and then pushed them aside with D9 bulldozers.

At 0014 on 9 November 2004, the advance elements of Task Force 2-7, Company C, 3d Battalion, 8th Cavalry, finally began to cross the berm following a tank with a plow and another with mine rollers. A section of tanks from Company C, 2d Tank Battalion, provided support-by-fire for the Army company's tanks and Bradleys, allowing them to move through the breach and establish a defensive outer ring. However, the lead elements of 3d Battalion, 1st Marines, that were advancing to Task Force 2-7's right ran into an unexpected obstacle: two-foot con-

Photo by LCpl Ryan B. Bussel

The D9 bulldozer was an important means for allowing Marines and soldiers to navigate and advance through Fallujah's urban terrain.

crete dividers that lined the city's northernmost road. The dividers kept the Marines from penetrating the city. As engineers worked to clear the dividers, they also blew another lane through the tracks and continued to improve the breach lanes for their wheeled vehicles.[79]

The conditions were difficult as the Marines and soldiers of Regimental Combat Team 1 waited to advance. "It was raining and it was a really miserable evening," recalled U.S. Army Major Timothy M. Karcher, Task Force 2-7's operations officer, "and we sat there for a good six or seven hours waiting to go, watching . . . death and destruction rain down on the city."[80] Lance Corporal Justin A. Boswood, team leader, 2d Platoon, Company K, 3d Battalion, 1st Marines, recalled, "We sat in tracs [amphibious assault vehicles] probably 8 to 10 hours, just waiting to roll in [with 25–30 Marines crammed in each]. And it started to rain, and you get cramped up, and you can't move your leg."[81] As advance forces of Task Force 2-7 and 3d Battalion, 1st Marines, methodically worked to open a breach into the city, AC-130H gunships attacked targets south of the train station and along Task Force 2-7's line of advance. The gunships worked to detonate IEDs and vehicleborne IEDs.[82]

Finally, at 0130, the remainder of Task Force 2-7 began moving through the breach. The heavy armor of Company C, 3d Battalion, 8th Cavalry, led Task Force 2-7's assault down Phase Line Henry. Through heavy small-arms and rocket-propelled grenade fire, the company quickly cut the north section of the city in half, isolating the enemy while destroying hastily made roadblocks and cars parked along the road—anything that appeared to be rigged as an IED. As Company C, 3d Battalion, 8th Cav-

alry, held its position, Task Force 2-7's Company C, 2d Battalion, 7th Cavalry, moved east and established support-by-fire locations oriented southward.[83] Task Force 2-7's movement through the breach was much slower than expected, as commanders had to guide their tanks and Bradleys on foot. Marines had, unfortunately, marked the breaching lanes and their vehicles with chem lights, which "were invisible to the thermal sights in our Bradleys," recalled U.S. Army Captain Christopher P. Brooke, Company C, 2d Battalion, 7th Cavalry's commanding officer.[84]

With Task Force 2-7's heavy armor penetrating into the city, Company K, 3d Battalion, 1st Marines, began moving into the city from the train station at 0400 behind a section of Marine tanks from Company C, 2d Tank Battalion, as Richard Wagner's "Ride of the Valkyries" blared from psychological operation's humvees.[85] Company I, 3d Battalion, 1st Marines, passed through the breach by 0600 with all of its attachments, while Company L followed the two lead companies in reserve without tanks.[86]

8 November: The Assault into Northeastern Fallujah

In Regimental Combat Team 7's sector, Colonel Tucker's three assault battalions began their breaching operations at 1900 on 8 November.[87] The 1st Battalion, 8th Marines, stood on the western flank; 1st Battalion, 3d Marines, in the center; and Task Force 2-2 occupied the assault force's eastern flank. D9 bulldozers pushed dirt over the railroad

Photo by LCpl Andrew D. Young

U.S. Army M2A3 Bradley Fighting Vehicles, such as the one pictured here cordoning off a road in ar-Ramadi in 2004, provided armored support to Marines and soldiers during the Second Battle of Fallujah.

20

Battle for Fallujah

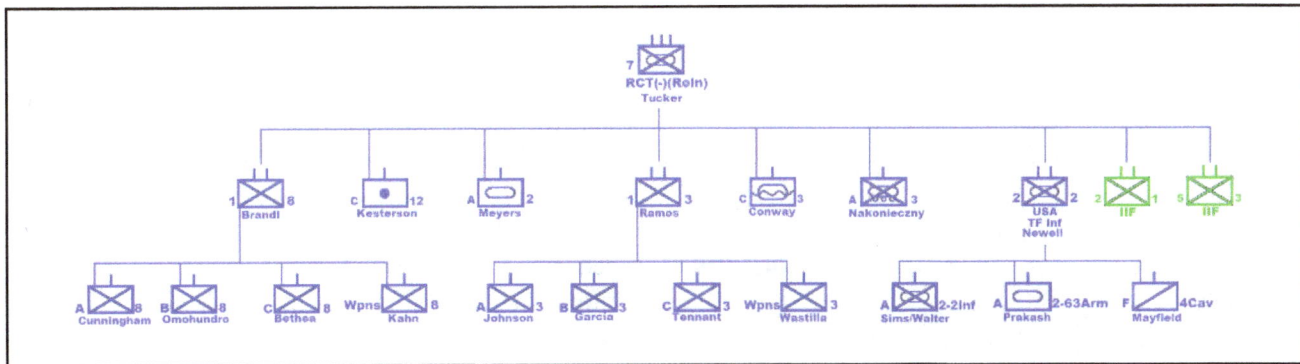

Diagram of Regimental Combat Team 7 during Operation al-Fajr.

tracks making ramps while engineers used mine-clearing line charges to clear IED lanes, triggering several series of secondary explosions. Bradleys from Task Force 2-2's brigade reconnaissance troop crossed flat terrain and breached the tracks first to provide support-by-fire.[88] Soon thereafter, at approximately 1940, the U.S. Army Bradleys of Company A, 2d Battalion, 2d Infantry, moved through the breach and came under enemy fire as they began clearing buildings. Company A, 2d Battalion, 63d Armored Cavalry, and the 2d Battalion, 1st Iraqi Intervention Force, followed and completed the breach at approximately 2151.[89] Unfortunately, enemy fire killed Task Force 2-2's command sergeant major, Steven W. Faulkenburg, USA, as he supervised the passing of vehicles into the breach lane.[90] Soon after, several of Task Force 2-2's Iraqi soldiers were injured by insurgent rockets and indirect fire from southern Fallujah. While doctors and medics worked on the arriving patients, insurgents attacked the logistics resupply point where the medical vehicles were located with rocket-propelled grenades.[91]

Meanwhile, engineers working with 1st Battalion, 8th Marines, succeeded in breaking the rails with mine-clearing line charges. One of the two D9 bulldozers that were to block the side roads and secure the companies' flanks became stuck in mud coming through the breach. As 1st Battalion, 8th Marines' Weapons Platoon engaged insurgents in the city from positions along the railroad tracks, amphibious tracked vehicles, tanks, and a mobile assault platoon provided support-by-fire while Company B, 1st Battalion, 8th Marines, went through the breach under fire and established a foothold within the city on the west side of Phase Line Ethan without incident. Once complete, the amphibious tracked vehicles returned to move Company C, 1st Battalion, 8th Marines, through the breach to seize a foothold on the east side of Phase Line Ethan. As the companies of Regimental Combat Team 7's main effort crossed the line of departure and moved into

the attack, Task Force High Value Target's SEAL and reconnaissance teams attached themselves to Companies B and C, 1st Battalion, 8th Marines. As Company C's executive officer, First Lieutenant Christopher S. Conner, observed, the task force's efforts had considerably eased 1st Battalion, 8th Marines' advance into the city. "The recon Marines had done an outstanding job in softening up targets for us on our initial footholds."[92]

Around 2200, both Company B and Company C, 1st Battalion, 8th Marines, began their attack dismounted. As the initial battalion main effort, Company C, reinforced with 86 Iraqi emergency response unit soldiers, 95 Iraqi security forces, and a force reconnaissance platoon, fought through determined insurgents and seized a suspected suicide belt factory. During the consolidation of the factory, a D9 bulldozer became stuck in mud, forcing Company C to leave one squad from 1st Platoon, which was protecting the company flanks and rear, with Iraqi soldiers from the 5th Battalion, 3d Brigade, 1st Iraq Intervention Force, to guard a second D9 and its crew.[93]

After midnight, it began to rain harder. This did not slow down the regiment's advance, however. Companies B and C, 1st Battalion, 8th Marines, continued to attack south down Phase Line Ethan, with Company C attacking down the eastern side toward the al-Hadrah al-Muhammadiyah Mosque and Company B, attacking down the west side toward the Islamic Culture Center across from the al-Hadrah Mosque. A platoon of tanks attacked down the center of the road. Both companies encountered heavy sniper fire and determined groups of insurgents who waited in ambush or attempted to maneuver behind them. Company C's commanding officer, Captain Theodore C. Bethea, ordered the weapons platoon and tank platoon to attack south along Phase Line Ethan in direct support of 2d Platoon, while 3d Platoon attacked south, adjacent to 2d Platoon. First Platoon protected the company's eastern flank. The company now

Photo by Cpl Theresa M. Medina

LtCol Gareth F. Brandl speaks with journalists on 19 November 2004. Brandl's 1st Battalion, 8th Marines, formed Regimental Combat Team 7's right flank as it advanced into eastern Fallujah.

formed a "U" shape that afforded maximum firepower to the front with the west flank guarded by tanks and the east flank guarded by 1st Platoon.[94]

As 1st Battalion, 8th Marines' assault companies attacked down Phase Line Ethan, their forward air control officers employed a Spectre gunship against pockets of insurgents.[95] The close-quarters nature of the combat in Fallujah made this a particularly challenging task. "Since the enemy was so close to us at that point, [the gunship] was having a hard time discerning who's friendly and who's not," remembered Company C executive officer Lieutenant Conner.[96] Captain Bethea had the lead tank mark Company C's forward trace, ordered all infrared strobe lights to be activated, and commanded the Marines to take cover. Ensuring that the Spectre could see the tank platoon on Phase Line Ethan and all friendly strobe lights, Captain Bethea authorized his forward air controller, Captain Travis R. Richie, to engage enemy forces within 60 meters with 40mm grenades. The AC-130H gunship confirmed that all enemy close to the company were de-

stroyed. Soon afterward, the gunship reported a larger enemy concentration gathering at a building 110 meters to the south of the company's lines. Captain Richie suggested to Captain Bethea that the AC-130H fire one 105mm round to ensure that it was targeting enemy forces and prevent possible fratricide. Captain Bethea approved the danger close mission, and the gunship engaged the enemy. The Spectre continued to strike reinforcements with the 105mm rounds as the enemy retreated south, and methodically destroyed 31 enemy forces along 2d Platoon, Company C's front.[97]

The first attempt by 1st Battalion, 3d Marines, to breach the railroad tracks with mine-clearing charges failed to create a passable lane in the center of Regimental Combat Team 7's line of advance. A pair of D9 bulldozers came up to push the train tracks out of the way and open the lane, but "the ground was so moist and the bulldozers so heavy, they both ended up getting stuck in the mud."[98] After several hours of trying to make the breach, 1st Battalion, 3d Marines' commanding officer, Lieutenant Colonel Michael R. Ramos, ordered Company C to dismount under fire and establish a foothold in the city. However, an amphibious assault vehicle struck an IED and triggered a daisy-chain of others that caused several casualties, further delaying the battalion's attack. Lieutenant Colonel Ramos used Task Force 2-2's breach to evacuate the wounded Marines and to move the tanks and equipment into the city. Company B also encountered problems breaching the tracks when its amphibious assault tractors arrived in the wrong order. The company then took them to the wrong breaching location, which forced them to reload the amphibious assault tractors under fire and move about a 100 meters down the berm.[99]

Once Company C, 1st Battalion, 3d Marines, dismounted their amphibious assault vehicles, the soldiers of the Iraqi Army's 5th Battalion, 3d Brigade, joined Company C just before moving through the breach. The Iraqis had taken heavy incoming fire after dismounting during the night, causing them to scatter for a time in the darkness until the Marine advisors pulled them together. Once Company C finally breached the berm with the Iraqi soldiers following behind, they established a foothold in alleys and homes about 50 meters into the city, then waited in the rain for the remainder of the battalion and its attachments to move through their breach site and assemble for the subsequent attack toward Phase Line Fran.[100] "After we set it and were there for about five minutes," Company C commanding officer Captain Thomas M. Tennant recalled, "we started taking sporadic small-arms fire. And Marines would return fire and when their return fire was accurate, the insurgents responded

Battle for Fallujah

Photo by LCpl Ryan B. Busse

Cpl Terry Cays of Combat Service Support Company 122 uses a sledgehammer to break through a wall as the 1st Marine Division advanced into Fallujah on 9 November 2004.

with mass fires. So their marksmanship was terrible but with rounds flying over your head it doesn't make you feel good. So Marines were engaging and killing insurgents in the dark at distances up to 150 meters."[101]

9 November: Regimental Combat Team 1's Continued Advance into the Jolan District

Before sunrise on 9 November, Company A, 2d Battalion, 7th Cavalry, moved from the train station behind Company C, 3d Battalion, 8th Cavalry, and then turned west to secure Jolan Park in northwestern Fallujah. At dawn, the company began its attack, using tanks and dismounted troops, and then cleared its rear. The attack "totally devastated the enemy" according to Task Force 2-7 commanding officer Lieutenant Colonel James E. Rainey, USA. He noted that "they were still trying to get out of the way of the tanks and the Bradleys and our infantry squads were on top of them."[102] With Jolan Park secure,

Rainey directed Company C, 2d Battalion, 7th Cavalry, to move down Phase Line Henry from its support-by-fire locations along Phase Line April. It started clearing buildings behind Company C, 3d Battalion, 8th Cavalry, which maintained heavy contact from teams of insurgents that attempted to counterattack from the rear as it held its position on Phase Line Henry at Phase Line Donna protecting Company A's eastern flank.[103]

As Company C, 2d Battalion, 7th Cavalry, moved in, it established support-by-fire locations oriented east and west along Phase Line Henry and similarly encountered heavy fighting with insurgents in the buildings and alleys along its route of advance. The 3d Battalion, 1st Marines, moved behind the heavy armor of Company C, 2d Battalion, 7th Cavalry, and began its assault. However, because the soldiers were in front, 3d Battalion, 1st Marines, could not use indirect fire on those insurgents who had hidden as the U.S. Army tanks and Bradleys passed and then came out to fight. As Company A, 2d Battalion, 7th Cavalry's soldiers waited for 3d Battalion, 1st Marines, at Jolan Park, they endured enemy sniper and rocket fire.[104]

By 0630 on the morning of 9 November, both Companies I and L, 3d Battalion, 5th Marines, had driven insurgents back into the city and neared the limits of their advance for the first day. Company K, 3d Battalion, 5th Marines, began moving to the Jolan cemetery in preparation for its attack, followed by the 1st Battalion, 1st Iraq Intervention Force, and Iraqi soldiers from the 1st Specialized Special Forces Battalion. At this point Marines confronted insurgents pretending to surrender only to continue fighting. As Company L waited for Companies I and K to get online, Company L Marines engaged a group of young men walking into the city from the countryside south of their position but stopped when they waved the white flag and appeared unarmed. "A few minutes after the men entered a building," recalled Company L commanding officer Eduardo C. Bitanga, "we started taking fire from that building and surrounding buildings. Because we [were] waiting for the battalion to get on line, we were unable to advance or maneuver on the enemy." Company L exchanged fire with the enemy from distances of 50–100 meters for about four hours and used M1A1 Abrams tanks and Super Cobra attack helicopters to destroy enemy positions until the enemy eventually stopped shooting. "We were unable to find the bodies of [the] enemy because the enemy had been policing their dead at night and moving them into buildings further south," Bitanga explained. "The next day we finally found bodies and knew that we were advancing faster than the enemy could react."[105]

Photo by LCpl Jason L. Andrade

LtCol Patrick J. Malay (pictured here in 2003 on the right) commanded the 3d Battalion, 5th Marines, during Operation al-Fajr. His battalion was tasked with clearing the heavily defended Jolan District of the city.

Once all three of its rifle companies were in the city, 3d Battalion, 5th Marines, began to advance through the Jolan District. As it did, the rapid push caused some insurgents to attempt to flee the city along the bank of the Euphrates River, where the boats of the Small Craft Company encountered them as the Marines evacuated their injured comrades from Company B, 1st Battalion, 23d Marines' fire support team. When the boats returned later, these insurgents had regrouped and attempted to ambush the boats as they sped by. The Small Craft Company would engage insurgents several times as the battle unfolded.[106]

With the attack underway and no reserve, Lieutenant Colonel Malay wanted 3d Battalion, 5th Marines, to begin detailed house-to-house, room-to-room clearing to prevent insurgents from rearming and refitting behind them. To accomplish this, 3d Battalion, 5th Marines' executive officer, Major Desgrosseilliers, assembled a second provisional task force, codenamed Task Force Bruno, built around a platoon of 40–50 Marines from Headquarters and Service Company and one section of the 81mm mortar platoon, two platoons of general support engineers,

explosive ordnance disposal Marines, two scout-sniper sections, a platoon of amphibian assault vehicles, several gun trucks, and a D9 bulldozer. The composition of Task Force Bruno often varied each day, depending on the needs of the battalion.[107]

Meanwhile, 3d Battalion, 1st Marines, fought its way south under sustained small-arms fire and mortar attacks to protect 3d Battalion, 5th Marine's left flank and catch up with Task Force 2-7.[108] Company K, 3d Battalion, 1st Marines' commanding officer Captain Timothy J. Jent recalled of the advance: "The company fought, primarily from north to south, with one tank platoon attached, two platoons up and one platoon back, fighting in the center with India Company on our eastern flank, and 3/5 on our western flank."[109] Captain Jent expanded on his company's operations, noting,

> We called it "fighting the box," which was two platoons up, kind of your combat trains in the middle, then you had a lighter platoon without tanks that would either provide security on a flank or would assist in CasEvac [casualty evac-

uation], kind of be that connecting file to the rear area if you can call it that. Then that was kind of our basic formation that we worked off and talked to and we used that the whole time.[110]

As 3d Battalion, 1st Marines, pushed through heavy fire and fortified positions, its tanks were attacked by insurgents. The insurgents attempted to disable the armor using rocket-propelled grenades against the tanks' tracks, bore evacuators, and optics. Around 0830, insurgents firing from behind a wall struck the bore evacuator on a tank commanded by Captain Bodisch, commanding officer of Company C, 2d Tank Battalion. The strike disabled the tank before it could fire on the insurgent forces.[111]

Meanwhile, Company L encountered heavy resistance from insurgents who had reentered buildings that Companies I and K had hastily searched. In one action, 1st Platoon, Company L, lost two Marines entering a house as insurgents waited in ambush. When Company L reached Phase Line Cathy, they came under heavy insurgent fire from mortars positioned underground and consequently hidden from the watchful eyes of the U.S. unmanned reconnaissance vehicles patrolling overhead.[112] At around 1200, Companies I and K, 3d Battalion, 5th Marines, advanced behind a platoon of Company C, 2d Tank Battalion's tanks while Captain Bitanga's Company L provided support-by-fire just north of the palm grove.

As the battle unfolded, one could see the different ways Marines and soldiers utilized their M1A1 and M1A2 tanks, with the key difference being that Marine tanks continuously accompanied Marine infantrymen during deliberate clearing operations, whereas Lieutenant Colonel Rainey's tanks generally held positions along the main line of communication after their initial assault.[113] "[Task Force] 2-7 wasn't much in the way of clearing," Major Timothy M. Karcher, Task Force 2-7's operations officer, explained. "We were in the mode of destroying. So the Marines [3d Battalion, 1st Marines] actually went in and did the dirty work of clearing, and I've got to give them credit for that. They were awesome, but they took a lot of casualties in the process."[114]

Once Companies I and K caught up to their tanks, Company L attacked into the palm grove. As Company K advanced behind their attached tanks, Captain Andrew J. McNulty used amphibious tracked vehicles to breach walls and humvees with chains to pull down gates and garage doors. Meanwhile, Company K's fire support team moved from rooftop to rooftop keeping direct fire and close air support in front of the company, reducing enemy strong points. "Every morning they would move into position and they would immediately begin to take fire up on the rooftop that they would use as their vantage point," recalled Captain McNulty, "and they would run deep fires and near fires throughout the zone, throughout the day, staying always just in front of the attacking platoons."[115] Both companies received sniper fire as they cleared the buildings in their sectors and uncovered multiple weapons caches along the way.[116]

Meanwhile, after advancing through the palm grove, Company L began searching homes along their avenue of attack. The company's 3d Platoon soon discovered a weapons cache inside a home. When the human exploitation team arrived to do the sensitive site exploitation, they heard noise coming from behind a wall and, after moving a safe, they found a passage into another room where they discovered a man chained to a wall. They also discovered bloodstains covering the walls in what appeared to be a torture and execution room that resembled the room where Abu Musab al-Zarqawi executed American businessman Nicholas Berg on 7 May 2004.[117]

Around 1230, 3d Battalion, 1st Marines, reached Phase Line Donna, where Company I completed a complex passage of the lines with Company A, 2d Battalion, 7th Cavalry, at Jolan Park, taking the battalion's southernmost position between Phase Line Donna and the street leading to the Old (or "Blackwater") Bridge. Company K remained in the center of the 3d Battalion, 1st Marines' line at Jolan Park, and Company L remained in place in the northernmost position of the battalion's line along Phase Line Cathy. Lieutenant Colonel Buhl's Marines were now online and reoriented to fight east to west. As the Marines of Company I held their objective on Phase Line Elizabeth, they endured nearly five hours of heavy insurgent small-arms and rocket-propelled grenade fire. During the afternoon, Captain Bodisch returned to combat with a new tank and promptly came to the aid of Company I Marines who had taken casualties from snipers in a building.[118]

After nearly 10 hours of fighting, 3d Battalion, 1st Marines, implemented an operational pause as it prepared for its assault the next morning. Company L, which had the difficult task of clearing buildings behind Companies I and K, had suffered most of the battalion's casualties on the first day of fighting. However, as the battalion held the position at Jolan Park, it continued to take mortar fire during the night. One mortar strike destroyed Company K commanding officer Captain Jent's vehicle. Marines also faced effective sniper fire that left one Marine and an Iraqi soldier dead. Company A, 2d Battalion, 7th Cavalry, remained at Jolan Park through the night as it prepared for its next mission and destroyed the large weapons cache it found on the scene.[119]

The Marines and soldiers advancing into Fallujah uncovered weapons caches throughout the city. Here a Marine from 3d Battalion, 1st Marines, carries a load of weapons found during the assault.

Around 1800 hours, 3d Battalion, 5th Marines, stopped their attack for the night while 3d Battalion, 1st Marines, remained abreast Phase Line Cathy at the Jolan Park. Five hours later Task Force 2-7's commanding officer, Lieutenant Colonel Rainey, launched Company C, 3d Battalion, 8th Cavalry Regiment, to attack the next objective, the Martyr's Cemetery along Phase Line Fran, which served as an insurgent command and control center. Rainey believed the lessons learned a few months earlier in an-Najaf—grab a piece of open terrain that would provide good fields of fire and kill the enemy while defending it—would work well for him here. Company C, 3d Battalion, 8th Cavalry, moved down Phase Line Henry, beyond the protection of Regimental Combat Team 7 on the eastern flank and 3d Battalion, 1st Marines, on the west and turned on Phase Line Fran toward the Martyr's Cemetery, again attacking through the objective, dismounting, and clearing back.[120] "We received sporadic sniper fire, mortar rounds, and RPGs [rocket-propelled grenades]," recalled U.S. Army Captain Peter C. Glass. "It didn't look like they had a defined defense. It looked like their defense got more elaborate as we pushed south.

When I secured that, I put a platoon in the west, a platoon in the east, and the infantry platoon had the inner cordon. They cleared all those schoolhouses in that area."[121] At one point, the soldiers came under fire from the adjacent mosque, which Apache helicopters from the 4th Aviation Brigade eventually neutralized after higher headquarters denied Glass's request for artillery or close air support. This move put Task Force 2-7 on the main supply route ahead of schedule. It also put Regimental Combat Team 1's assault battalions in a good position for the next day's attack.[122]

9 November: Regimental Combat Team 7's Continued Assault through the Northeast

At the same time that Regimental Combat Team 1's three battalions were advancing gradually southwest, Colonel Tucker's Regimental Combat Team 7 advanced southward to clear the eastern section of the city to Phase Line Fran (Highway 10). On Regimental Combat Team 7's

An M1A1 Abrams from 2d Tank Battalion attached to 1st Battalion, 8th Marines, waits for personnel and vehicles (such as the M1114 High-Mobility Multipurpose Wheeled Vehicle [HMMWV] to its right) to move away before it fires on a suspected insurgent position in Fallujah. Both types of vehicles gave the 1st Marine Division the mobility and power needed to rapidly sweep across the city.

eastern flank, Task Force 2-2's heavy armor and mechanized infantrymen had rapidly moved during the night through fortified positions and tenacious groups of insurgents along the city's eastern edge.

As the sun came up, however, Task Force 2-2's soldiers began to take heavy fire from the southern half of the city, past Phase Line Fran.[123] "We were going to set up a hasty defense there and conduct a tactical pause to refit," recalled U.S. Army Captain Jeffrey R. Emery, 1st Platoon leader, Company A, 2d Battalion, 2d Infantry, "but it didn't quite work out, because once daylight hit and we were trying to get set up, we started taking pretty heavy fire."[124] Captain Emery noted the effectiveness and precision of the insurgent attacks. "We got up there [Phase Line Fran], took some fire, dropped off dismounts in the buildings and cleared so they could get a foothold and get in the fight, too, and once that happened, RPGs [rocket-propelled grenades] were just being launched from the south side of Highway 10 and they were fairly accurate. They were actually impacting the buildings where we had dismounted troops and were impacting pretty close to the vehicles."[125]

However, while the insurgent fire was persistent, it was not organized and it was clear to the soldiers of Task Force 2-2 that the rapidity of their assault had caught the insurgents by surprise. Captain Neil S. Prakash, USA, whose Company A, 2d Battalion, 63d Armored Cavalry, had reached Phase Line Fran around 0900 hours, recalled, "It seemed that we really advanced faster than the enemy expected, and they were falling back to regroup. They weren't ready yet to stand toe-to-toe."[126]

In the center on Regimental Combat Team 7's line, 1st Battalion, 3d Marines' companies waited in the homes and alleys taking sporadic fire for about two hours before being given the order to move out just before dawn.[127] Just after sunrise on 9 November, however, 1st Battalion, 3d Marines, came into heavy contact with groups of insurgents, many fleeing Task Force 2-2's rapid assault on their eastern flank. Captain Garcia recalled, "We're reorganizing, making sure everybody's there. Sun starts [to rise], and it's just quiet, dead quiet. . . . As the sun started rising, we just started receiving small arms and rocket-propelled grenade [rocket-propelled grenades] just out of every-

Photo by Cpl Joel A. Chaverri

GySgt Ryan P. Shane (center) and another Marine from 1st Battalion, 8th Marines, recover a fatally wounded Marine while under enemy fire during the Second Battle of Fallujah.

where, out of every nook and cranny."[128] As the battalion came in contact, 1st Battalion, 3d Marines, fought quickly through insurgents, attacking to protect 1st Battalion, 8th Marines' flank. Company C, 1st Battalion, 3d Marines, advanced down the battalion center, Company A advanced along the battalion's right, and Company B moved on the left along Task Force 2-2's axis of advance.[129]

Approximately 150 meters into the city, Company C, 1st Battalion, 3d Marines, killed several insurgents as they came upon the al-Tawfiq Mosque and suppressed rocket-propelled grenade fire with main tank rounds. A small group of Iraqi soldiers from the 5th Battalion, 3d Brigade, Iraqi Army, led by Marine advisor Captain Brian T. Mulvihill, cleared the mosque after tank fire breached the compound walls. Although the Marine advisors were not supposed to lead the Iraqis, most of the Iraqis would not cross the open field in the face of machine-gun fire, and those that did had to be prompted by Marines.[130] Once inside the compound, Company C came up to the mosque with the remaining Iraqis, and discovered weapons that had been discarded and others partially

broken down in solvent, indicating that Marines likely caught them by surprise and forced them to flee in a hurry.[131] Company C remained at the mosque with the Iraqi soldiers to rest before moving toward their next objective. During this time, Company C commanding officer Captain Tennant asked a U.S. Army sergeant from the psychological operations section to use the mosque speakers to broadcast a surrender message. The insurgents only responses came in the form of rocket-propelled grenades and small-arms fire.[132] On the west of Colonel Tucker's line, 1st Battalion, 8th Marines' Companies B and C prepared for their attack down Phase Line Ethan.

Task Force High Value Target's SEAL and reconnaissance teams decided to move out on their own about 500 meters ahead of the companies to get good support-by-fire positions to prevent insurgents from moving across the seam and between 1st Battalion, 8th Marines, and 1st Battalion, 3d Marines. However, when artillery fired a white phosphorous smoke mission to screen 1st Battalion, 8th Marines' advance, the projectiles landed around

Battle for Fallujah

Photo by Sgt Jonathan C. Knauth

Marines from Regimental Combat Team 7 prepare to attack insurgents inside a Fallujah mosque on 10 November 2004.

Task Force High Value Target teams, which covered their movement but also slightly injured some members of the team. These deadly projectiles also exploded over Company B, 1st Battalion, 8th Marines, forcing them to fall back. Meanwhile, one of 1st Battalion, 8th Marines' tanks encountered an errant U.S. Army tank moving toward it on Phase Line Ethan, which fired in its direction before the Marines of 1st Battalion, 8th Marines, made contact with it and escorted it out of its zone.[133]

Once 1st Battalion, 8th Marines' companies moved out they started receiving intense small-arms fire from their west. The battalion believed this was actually friendly fire from Regimental Combat Team 1 directed at insurgents fighting between the two assault regiments. Companies B and C subsequently waited at their positions until it was over.[134] After that, both rifle companies faced increasing resistance along Phase Line Ethan as they closed on their objectives, battling through machine-gun fire, snipers, and a large number of insurgents. They also encountered IEDs, including a vehicleborne IED, and a suicide bomber with an explosive vest who blew himself up trying to kill Marines. Company A, 1st Battalion, 8th Marines,

was to begin its assault on the Fallujah government center a few hours later during the early morning of 9 November, but Lieutenant Colonel Brandl decided to delay its assault to allow Companies B and C to reach and secure their objectives.[135]

Company B, 1st Battalion, 8th Marines, began its assault on the Islamic Cultural Center by crossing a six-lane road where it endured heavy machine-gun and sniper fire. Once across the dangerous road, Company B's Marines secured the Islamic Cultural Center by 0900, then waited to support Company C's assault on the al-Hadrah Mosque. Company B's Marines found numerous weapons, munitions, and IED-making material inside the Islamic Cultural Center.[136]

At about 1030 hours, Company C, 1st Battalion, 8th Marines, and the Iraqi emergency response unit assaulted the al-Hadrah Mosque as Company B provided support from the Islamic Cultural Center. To direct his company's assault, Captain Bethea, his first sergeant, and the Iraqi emergency response unit liaison officers maneuvered under fire to the second floor and then to the roof of the last concealed position across the street from the al-

Hadrah Mosque. Captain Bethea directed the tanks to destroy the enemy sniper and small-arms fire positions located east of the mosque while coordinating with the Iraqi emergency response unit liaison officer to determine the best locations to breach the mosque walls. Captain Bethea ordered the tanks to fire main gun rounds and create three breach holes along the mosque's north wall, create two breaches along the west wall, and destroy potential vehicleborne IEDs outside of the mosque.

Captain Bethea then ordered one tank to establish a battle position oriented to the east and another tank to establish a battle position oriented to the south. Once the tanks were in position, he ordered 2d Platoon of Company B to throw smoke grenades to conceal the Iraqi emergency response unit's subsequent assault. Simultaneously, the emergency response unit soldiers followed their liaison officers through the smoke screen into the al-Hadrah Mosque. Once inside, the unit discovered rocket-propelled grenades, hand grenades, rifles, AK47s, bloody load-bearing vests, and AK47 magazines. The back of the mosque contained an infirmary with several beds, a dead insurgent in a bed, and medication.[137] In the Islamic Cultural Center across the street from the al-Hadrah Mosque, Company B's Marines found numerous weapons, munitions, and IED-making material.[138]

As it held its position on Company C, 1st Battalion, 8th Marines' flank, Task Force High Value Target's Team 1 suffered two casualties as it fought with insurgents. Company C also suffered two casualties from snipers as it evacuated Team 1's Marines.[139] The task force's forward air control officer, Major David C. Morris, recalled the difficulty of extracting the Marines: "The problem was that we didn't know where everybody was. So we couldn't call in CAS [close air support], because we'd get on the top of the building and I look over, 100 meters to our east, there's a squad of Marines setting on the top of a building. I look up 150 meters to my northwest, and there's another squad of Marines . . . I look up a couple 100 meters to the north, and there's another group of Marines on the building."[140]

Further east, Company C, 1st Battalion, 3d Marines, advanced toward the Mujahareen Mosque with Company B on its east and Iraqi soldiers and Company A following behind. As the company moved, it came under fire from small groups of insurgents on the side streets.[141] "Literally every single step of the way," recalled Captain Tennant, "we were engaging the enemy."[142] Upon securing the Mujahareen Mosque, Company C moved to the Lucia Harim Mosque, about 200 meters away. As Marines crossed a wide multilane road under fire, Captain Tennant recalled, "I stepped out into the street and I saw bul-

U.S. Army Task Force 2-2 provided Regimental Combat Team 7 with an armored, highly mobile unit for its assault on eastern Fallujah. The task force was commanded by LtCol Peter A. Newell, pictured here as a colonel in 2010.

lets marking the ground as I ran. I mean literally bouncing off the street in front of me as I took steps across the street." Once across the street, Tennant recalled, "We started to clear some buildings to redistribute ammo, drink some water, throw some chow down real fast, catch our breath, and push the tanks up to get a visual on what the objective looked like."[143]

Advisors Captain Mulvihill and Staff Sergeant Anthony Villa led Iraqi soldiers into the mosque compound to secure it. "It was daytime now, and the Iraqis were a little more willing to fight," Mulvihill recalled. "They had some confidence now that they saw the Marines who were killing people, that no Iraqis were hurt or killed yet. . . . It still took me and Staff Sergeant Villa being the first ones into the compound and leading them in again. Shouldn't be doing that, but we had to at this point."[144]

Meanwhile, Task Force 2-2's Company A, 2d Battalion, 2d Infantry, and Company A, 2d Battalion, 63d Armor, realigned their forces and gained better observation points and fighting positions. They began to engage insurgents with indirect fire, as Task Force 2-2's engineers cleared Main Supply Route Michigan of IEDs. In one instance, as Company A, 2d Battalion, 63d Armor's tanks sat on Phase Line Fran coordinating indirect fire on insurgent positions in the industrial district, company commander Captain Prakash ordered artillery fire on a building next to a mosque after observing groups of insurgents running into it.[145] Following a 20-round bombardment, insurgents came stumbling outside, coughing from the smoke. Prakash subsequently ordered a second bombardment.[146]

After Company A, 2d Battalion, 2d Infantry's soldiers had neutralized insurgents fighting along Phase Line Fran, the soldiers attacked 300 meters into the industrial district, securing an entry into the city for resupply and medical evacuation, and then waited for the regiment's two remaining battalions to finish clearing buildings and catch up. Newell then directed his soldiers to clear the buildings behind them that they had bypassed during their rapid assault to Phase Line Fran. He also used the opportunity to cycle his tanks and vehicles back for fuel and allow his soldiers some sleep. Throughout the day, Company A, 2d Battalion, 2d Infantry, along with 2d Battalion, 1st Iraq Intervention Force, conducted search-and-attack missions in northeastern Fallujah. The Iraqi soldiers engaged a determined group of insurgents, and Newell was forced to send two tanks back to support them.[147]

In the center of Regimental Combat Team 7's line, 1st Battalion, 3d Marines, encountered bands of insurgents fleeing Task Force 2-2's rapid assault. As the insurgents attacked, speakers on a nearby mosque broadcast anti-U.S. propaganda. As the battalion's commander, Lieutenant Colonel Ramos, later recalled, "I'll never forget it as long as I live; the chanting that was going on. It was tribal, it was savage, it was intense, and it was—it was scary. I wanted to destroy that mosque."[148] One of the battalion's interpreters revealed that the recording declared "Citizens of Fallujah, stand up, the infidels are here. Kill them, kill them all."[149] After a short respite, Company C, 1st Battalion, 3d Marines, resumed their attack on the structure itself where Marines cleared buildings around the mosque, and Iraqi soldiers cleared the actual building. Afterward, Captain Tennant sent a patrol to search a parking lot east of the mosque where Company C discovered a large weapons cache and 20-foot tractor-trailer containers full of different weapons. During this search, Captain Tennant's Marines witnessed a gruesome sight: "Almost as soon as these insurgents were dead," Captain Tennant explained, "the dogs started gnawing on their bones."[150] Meanwhile, Captain Garcia's Company B, 1st

Battalion, 3d Marines, had reached Phase Line Fran around 1330 hours, and the remainder of Lieutenant Colonel Ramos' battalion reached the position before nightfall on 9 November.[151] At this point, Captain Lee A. Johnson's Company A, 1st Battalion, 3d Marines, moved across Phase Line Fran, and began clearing the homes and buildings in their objective area.[152]

After a day of hard fighting, Colonel Tucker's three assault battalions held for the night. Meanwhile, Spectre gunships worked throughout the night to kill insurgents attempting to maneuver, which allowed the soldiers and Marines of both regiments to rest.[153] By the end of the day on 9 November, the relentless bombing successfully eroded the insurgents' command and cohesion, which allowed soldiers and Marines to advance rapidly through parts of the city. As expected, soldiers and Marines encountered concentrations of insurgent forces in fortified positions during their first day of combat, along with snipers, rocket-propelled grenade teams, and indirect fire. However, the assault force's rapid penetration into the city and overwhelming firepower had quickly eroded enemy defenses. Many insurgents began to fall back into the city, while others hid as the Marines and armor passed by, hoping to attack from behind. "The rapid penetration by U.S. Army's heavy armor completely fractured the enemy's defenses and the sudden deep penetration behind their lines caused a psychological blow," Lieutenant Colonel Buhl observed, "They [insurgents] never were able to really coordinate defenses, especially when we applied our combined arms against them."[154]

The Third Day: Regimental Combat Team 1 from the Jolan District to the Euphrates River

Before dawn on 10 November 2004, Company C, 3d Battalion, 8th Cavalry, moved west along Phase Line Fran from its position at the Martyr's Cemetery to cover the area surrounding Fallujah's two bridges spanning the Euphrates.

"From our experience in Najaf," recalled company commander Captain Glass, "we knew that the enemy didn't fight at night. They tended to hunker down and gather themselves and rest. So we used the cover of darkness to get behind their lines."[155] About the same time, Company A, 2d Battalion, 7th Cavalry, moved back to the train station from the Jolan Park to refit, rearm, and refuel. While refitting, the company's commanding officer, Captain Edward S. Twaddell III, USA, received orders to conduct reconnaissance of the two bridges.[156]

Photo by LCpl Ryan L. Jones

Marines from 3d Battalion, 1st Marines, advance through the Jolan District during the initial assault into Fallujah on 9 November 2004.

As the sun came up, 3d Battalion, 1st Marines, attacked west, passing in front of 3d Battalion, 5th Marines. Company K attacked west toward the al-Kabir Mosque as forward observers fired artillery about 100 meters ahead of Company K's advancing Marines, clearing IEDs and rooftops along the way.[157] "As soon as the sun came up," recalled First Lieutenant John Jacobs, platoon commander of 2d Platoon, Company K, 3d Battalion, 1st Marines, "they started hitting the area around the mosque with artillery and they dropped two 500-pound bombs."[158] The attack destroyed the buildings surrounding the mosques, which were full of explosives, but as Lieutenant Colonel Buhl noted, the mosque itself was left "completely intact."[159]

The artillery was effective in chasing insurgents from the area, and many attempted to swim across the river where 3d Battalion, 1st Marines' forward observers killed them with artillery fire. Major Christeon C. Griffin, the battalion's operations officer, recalled that the attack toward the Euphrates River "was largely uncontested . . . the artillery really facilitated some rapid maneuver to the west."[160] Company L fought through several groups of in-

surgents, including a barrage of hand grenades, as it moved between Phase Line Cathy and Phase Line Donna toward its company objectives, a water treatment facility and a school on the banks of the Euphrates River. In one case, Company L used white phosphorous smoke to screen its movement and dislodge insurgents hiding in the palm groves along the river.[161]

The 3d Battalion, 1st Marines' three-hour move westward adversely affected 3d Battalion, 5th Marines' ability to put indirect fires to the south.[162] As it waited for 3d Battalion, 1st Marines, to cross in front on Phase Line Cathy, 3d Battalion, 5th Marines, conducted a boundary shift after dawn that brought them between the Euphrates River and Phase Line Jacob, so they were able to attack south through the Jolan District. When 3d Battalion, 5th Marines, finally began its assault, Company L advanced through heavy insurgent rocket-propelled grenade and indirect fire along the river and seized the Abu Ayyub al-Ansar Mosque and other key terrain just south of Phase Line Beth. At the same time, Company K maneuvered down the center and Company I moved down the eastern flank.[163] During their assault along the river, the third pla-

Battle for Fallujah

Marines from the 3d Battalion, 5th Marines, pause in their advance into Fallujah on 12 November 2004. They are standing in front of an M1114 High-Mobility Multipurpose Wheeled Vehicle.

toon from the battalion's Company L killed three insurgents inside a house. One Marine was wounded in the fight. Soon afterward, Company L's Marines engaged a large group of insurgents behind the house in the marshes just north of the bend in the river. These insurgents had earlier ambushed the small craft company attempting to pass and began to advance on Company L for about 20 minutes until the rifle company's forward observers directed heavy 81mm mortar fire on them.[164]

Confident that the insurgents could not launch a counterattack, Lieutenant Colonel Malay deployed his full battalion in full force, without reserves.[165] Soon after beginning its assault, however, 3d Battalion, 5th Marines, came under fire from insurgent snipers in buildings and rocket-propelled grenade teams on the streets, suffering several casualties. They also encountered complex, in-depth defenses with mutually supporting fields of fire, ambushes in courtyards, and well-trained foreign fighters. The 3d Battalion, 5th Marines, quickly returned fire and attacked enemy strong points as Marine and SEAL sniper teams provided overwatch and support-by-fire. As

Marines entered the buildings, the fighting became intense and close when they encountered machine guns and fortified positions. November 10 would be the heaviest day of fighting for 3d Battalion, 5th Marines.[166]

Deploying its combined antiarmor team forward to screen the road ahead, Company K attacked with three platoons. Company K's Marines soon discovered eight Iraqi bodies in the street that were believed to have been executed: seven were shot in the head and one had his feet cut off.[167] As Company K moved south, they located and destroyed two insurgent observation posts. As they drew closer to Phase Line Cathy, they came into contact with different insurgent sniper and rifle-propelled grenade teams in the streets immediately north of 3d Battalion, 1st Marines' positions.

In the early afternoon, 3d Battalion, 5th Marines, was finishing the day's attack through the Jolan District while 3d Battalion, 1st Marines, held blocking positions about two blocks south along Phase Line Cathy, preventing the enemy from escaping south.[168] Meanwhile, around 0900, Company A, 2d Battalion, 7th Cavalry, left the train sta-

A CH-46E Sea Knight helicopter from Marine Medium Helicopter Squadron 268 performs a casualty evacuation for 3d Battalion, 5th Marines, on 10 November 2004. Marine rotary-wing assets provided critical support throughout Operation al-Fajr.

tion to monitor the city's main bridge. The company moved south down Phase Line Henry to Phase Line Fran, then moved west across Phase Line Fran, past Captain Glass's Company C, 3d Battalion, 8th Cavalry Regiment, to the new bridge and eliminated a squad-size element of insurgent defenders in a short engagement. The company conducted a visual reconnaissance of the bridge but did not cross it due to concerns that the span was booby-trapped with improvised explosives. These concerns were shown to be legitimate, as it was discovered that insurgents had dug holes in the bridge in which they placed mines and then covered them up with asphalt or melted tires.[169] With the bridge secure, Company A, 2d Battalion, 7th Cavalry Regiment, then attacked north along the river road to the northern bridge, quickly defeating another 10 to 15 insurgents, and then assumed overwatch positions until 3d Battalion, 1st Marines, came in to secure and hold the bridges.[170]

Regimental Combat Team 1's advance unfolded according to plan. As the 3d Battalion, 5th Marines, proceeded south, the other two battalions had pivoted

westward, with the 3d Battalion, 1st Marines, advancing across the middle of the Jolan District and Task Force 2-7 moving toward the two Euphrates bridges. Meanwhile, the 4th Iraq Intervention Force moved along the regiment's eastern flank to screen for insurgents fleeing westward in the face of Regimental Combat Team 7's attack. Another Iraqi force, the 1st Iraq Intervention Force, conducted house-to-house search-and-clear operations in the regiment's rear.[171] The latter force, working alongside 3d Battalion, 5th Marines' Task Force Bruno, uncovered significant numbers of ammunition and weapons caches. The battalion operations officer, Major Desgrosseilliers, recalled, "They'd go into a house and find stuff a lot quicker than we would."[172]

Company K, 3d Battalion, 1st Marines, fought to secure the al-Kabir Mosque while Companies I and L secured the school and water treatment facility along the Euphrates River. Company L endured friendly artillery fire at its position at the school as forward observers continued calling fire on insurgents attempting to flee along the river. With their objective secure, Companies I and L then

Battle for Fallujah

A Marine (left) from Company I, 3d Battalion, 5th Marines, and an Iraqi soldier search a room in Fallujah during Operation al-Fajr.

cleared areas along the Euphrates River. Company K finished securing the al-Kabir Mosque around 1600 hours, having discovered several small weapons caches in the process. After sweeping across the Jolan District between Phase Line Cathy and Phase Line Elizabeth, 3d Battalion, 1st Marines, ended the day's assault and established company defensive positions for the evening.[173]

Just north of 3d Battalion, 1st Marines, 3d Battalion, 5th Marines, began to engage a determined enemy occupying fortified positions inside homes, hoping to draw Marines into their kill zones. These kill zones included courtyards, rooms, and hallways, where insurgents skillfully employed machine guns, rocket-propelled grenades, and assorted small arms to ambush Marines using mutually supporting fire. In eliminating these strong points, the Marines faced intense squad-level house-to-house fighting that would characterize the nature of fighting throughout the rest of the battle.

Indicative of this fighting was a series of simultaneous engagements that Company K, 3d Battalion, 5th Marines, found itself in. At around 1300 hours, the first squad of Company K's 3d Platoon encountered a fireteam-size el-

ement of insurgents manning a hardened RPK machine-gun position inside a building as the squad leader, Sergeant Jeffrey L. Kirk, opened the gate leading into the courtyard and began to lead his squad toward the building. Only steps into the courtyard, an insurgent threw a grenade at Kirk. Upon hearing their squad leader shout "grenade!" Kirk's Marines quickly withdrew outside the courtyard and moved away to a corner of the courtyard concealed from the doorway. Cut off from his Marines, Kirk found himself behind a narrow pillar that offered little protection. On his right was a window into the building that he could not see through, but he believed the enemy could see him—and behind him was another door into the building.[174]

Believing it his best chance for survival, Kirk bolted through the gate to rejoin his Marines, evading machine-gun fire. He then organized a new assault on the building. Seconds later, Kirk threw a grenade into the building just as an insurgent threw one at him, but the insurgent's grenade did not go off. Kirk then led his Marines into the courtyard, moving left of the machine-gun fire, and threw another grenade into the building before making entry amid the smoke of the grenades. However, the machine-gun fire forced Sergeant Kirk and his men to withdraw. Kirk attacked the room a second time with grenades and M16A4 rifle fire and was shot in the buttocks as he entered the doorway. Despite his wound, Sergeant Kirk killed the insurgent machine-gunner. However, other insurgents in the building opened fire and threw grenades, which forced Sergeant Kirk and his Marines to withdraw again. As they fell back, Kirk and his Marines continued to fire and throw grenades at the insurgents, killing some of them. Although he was wounded, Sergeant Kirk refused medical attention and made 10 individual assaults on the building until he and his Marines finally succeed in killing all of the insurgents and clearing the building.

During Sergeant Kirk's firefight, elements of 3d Platoon and the combined antiarmor team section supporting the company came into contact about two blocks ahead of Company K's advance. Meanwhile, Lance Corporal Ryan W. Sunnerville's fire team from 1st squad, 1st Platoon, finished clearing a building after killing an insurgent with a rocket-propelled grenade and finding a large weapons cache, and moved toward the next building. As he did, Lance Corporal Erick J. Hodges killed an insurgent on the road with his squad automatic weapon before entering the next compound. Hodges led the fireteam through the gate and cut diagonally right across the courtyard toward the first door he spotted, with Sunnerville following behind. After finding the first door locked, Hodges moved around the left corner of the building back into the courtyard toward the second door where he was cut down by enemy machine-gun fire coming from a loophole in the wall next to the doorway. Sunnerville and Hospital Corpsman Alonso A. Rogero were also wounded. The remainder of Sunnerville's fireteam took cover behind the wall of the house near the first closed door.

Corporal Jeremy M. Baker, a fireteam leader from 2d Squad, 1st Platoon, was on the road outside the compound and saw the fireteam huddled in the corner and ran through the kill zone to support them amid enemy machine-gun fire. Private First Class Christopher S. Adlesperger told Baker that Hodges had been hit and was dead just before insurgents in the building threw grenades and fired on the Marines. Both Baker and Adlesperger used their own bodies to shield Rogero and Sunnerville from the fragmentation.[175]

Corporal Baker saw a ladder well to the rooftop and ordered Adlesperger to clear both it and the rooftop. Once cleared, Baker and Adlesperger helped move Sunnerville and Rogero to the roof. Adlesperger threw a fragmentation grenade into the courtyard and Sunnerville threw a grenade toward the ladder well, but it hit the wall and bounced back within two meters of them. Baker and Adlesperger immediately grabbed Sunnerville and Rogero and pulled them to cover behind a wall on the L-shaped roof. The grenade detonated and there were no further injuries. While changing magazines on his M16A4, Adlesperger saw two insurgents run toward the ladder well. He then threw a grenade down, forcing one insurgent to expose himself, and Adlesperger shot him; he forced the other to run into the street where Marines immediately killed him.[176]

Outside the compound, the company came under heavy sniper, small-arms, and rocket-propelled grenade fire, which pinned down 1st Platoon's commander and his machine-gun team. As Captain McNulty and a SEAL sniper team moved to a rooftop immediately southwest of Adlesperger's position to gain observation and provide support-by-fire, they observed Adlesperger shooting down on insurgents with an M203 40mm grenade launcher through a barred window. Although the distance did not give Adlesperger's grenades time to arm, the actions did flush out insurgents. Adlesperger then saw three insurgents run into the courtyard directly below and promptly killed two of them. He then shot the third insurgent who paused to look up at him while attempting to steal the gun sight from Lance Corporal Hodges's M249 squad automatic weapon and then returned to Baker's position, where he had triaged and stabilized the casualties. Meanwhile, another squad moved from rooftop to rooftop toward Adlesperger's position and found the wall separating the buildings too high to climb over. The squad then pushed the wall over with their shoulders and helped evacuate the wounded.[177]

An amphibious tracked vehicle arrived and fired .50-caliber machine-gun rounds into the building, which set off a weapons cache and started a fire in the house. Soon afterward Captain McNulty arrived with the platoon sergeant and Corporal Terrance J. Van Doorn's 3d Squad and received a situation report. He then ordered 3d Squad, Corporal Baker, and Private First Class Adlesperger to set a support-by-fire position on a rooftop to the south. However, after clearing the house they found that the rooftop wall was too high. The squad came back to McNulty where they used the amphibious tracked vehicle to break down the side gate. McNulty's team donned their gas masks, and Adlesperger and Baker threw high-concentrate smoke into the buildings to suffocate insurgents before McNulty threw fragmentation grenades. Baker, Adlesperger, and McNulty assaulted the building and destroyed the remaining insurgents. After securing the

Battle for Fallujah

LtCol Michael R. Ramos (center), the commander of 1st Battalion, 3d Marines, speaks with an Iraqi during Operation al-Fajr.

building, Company K, 3d Battalion, 5th Marines, moved through the broken gate and rubble to recover Hodges and discovered residue from gunshots on back of his head, indicating that he had been shot at close range.[178] Private Adlesperger would be killed a month later, on 9 December, while clearing another house in Fallujah. He would receive the Navy Cross for his actions on 10 November 2004.

The battalion's Companies I and L similarly encountered heavy resistance from a determined enemy as they advanced toward Phase Line Cathy, including 81mm mortar fire.[179] Once 3d Battalion, 5th Marines, finally eliminated enemy strong points in the Jolan District, they continued to search and clear buildings as they moved toward Phase Line Cathy. As they cleared homes, they discovered numerous weapons caches, civilians inside homes, and insurgents surrendering. After a full day of fighting, 3d Battalion, 5th Marines, finally reached Phase Line Cathy and stopped its assault to rest and recover for the evening.

10 November: Regimental Combat Team 7 Seizes the Government Center

In Regimental Combat Team 7's sector, Company A, 1st Battalion, 8th Marines, left the line of departure in amphibious assault vehicles at 0400 hours to begin its assault on the government center. They advanced rapidly down Ethan, turned west on Phase Line Cathy at the al-Hadrah Mosque, then finally advanced south again on Phase Line Frank, reaching the government center. Company A's attached tanks and amphibious assault vehicles breached the compound wall in several locations. Marines then dismounted, entered the compound, and set up a 360-degree security perimeter before assaulting the buildings with shoulder-launched, multipurpose assault weapons to get into the buildings. As they penetrated deeper into the compound, however, they confronted two lines of enemy defenses, one inside the compound and a second across Main Supply Route Michigan. Defeating these insurgent lines would occupy 1st Battalion, 8th Marines, for the next 36 hours.[180]

Photo by SSgt Jonathan C. Knauth

Marine SSgt Scott Perry (left) and another Marine of Company B, 1st Battalion, 8th Marines, throw grenades into an insurgent stronghold.

As the sun came up, Company A, 1st Battalion, 8th Marines, had secured the government center on Phase Line Fran. With Company A now occupying the government center, Company B attacked the nearby Iraqi National Guard complex. During the assault, Company B's Marines came under sniper fire from the minarets of a mosque on Phase Line Fran, requiring AH-1 Cobra attack helicopters to attack the minarets around 0930 hours with Maverick and Hellfire missiles. Once Company B secured the Iraqi National Guard complex, Company B commanding officer Captain Read M. Omohundro sent a platoon across Phase Line Fran to secure a five-story building from which insurgents had been attacking on the rooftop. Once insurgents realized where Marines were firing from, Company B's Marines endured a lengthy engagement with insurgents for the rest of the day as observers from the company's fire support team coordinated artillery on the attacking insurgents. Meanwhile, Company C continued to hold at the al-Hadrah Mosque and continued to encounter snipers and bands of maneuvering insurgents.[181]

In the center of Regimental Combat Team 7's line, 1st Battalion, 3d Marines, began clearing areas in its sector they had bypassed the day before.[182] "We never really got a formal order at that point to begin searching house-to-house," company commander Captain Tennant recalled, "but tactically it made sense to me to make sure that nobody crept up to get right close next to [Company C] to ambush or even just to gain intelligence about what we were doing."[183] As they searched, 1st Battalion, 3d Marines, soon discovered numerous weapons caches, new military equipment, and drugs. They also battled groups of insurgents waiting in ambush for them.

These ambushes demonstrated the challenges Marines faced as they cleared Fallujah's structures one by one. In another example, one of Company C's squads cleared the first floor of a building. As they advanced up the stairs, insurgents killed Lance Corporal Aaron C. Pickering and wounded the other Marines who were with him. The enemy forces commenced firing armor-piercing rounds through the floor at the Marines below, pinning them under the stairwell, and threw grenades down the stairs. The remainder of Company C came to the squad's rescue and attempted to extract the trapped Marines through windows and walls. During the rescue attempts, insur-

Battle for Fallujah

gents killed Hospital Corpsman 3d Class Julian Woods when he tried to enter through the front door. Finally, Captain Tennant sent a D9 bulldozer to the platoon commander, First Lieutenant Dustin M. Shumney, who used it to knock down a wall and free his embattled Marines.[184]

On the other side of Phase Line Fran, Company A, 1st Battalion, 3d Marines, continued clearing homes and buildings with Iraqi soldiers. During the operation, an insurgent pretending to be dead shot a U.S. Army advisor in the head. With many Iraqi units already short of advisors, Company A commander Captain Johnson gave his executive officer and a radio operator to the Iraqi unit and then used the unit as one of his own platoons.[185]

On Regimental Combat Team 7's east flank, Company A, 2d Battalion, 2d Infantry, continued clearing buildings north of Phase Line Fran and encountered a determined enemy that fought from occupied buildings. In one encounter, U.S. Army Staff Sergeant David Bellavia's platoon engaged several insurgents in a fierce close-quarters battle that injured several soldiers. In an effort to save his wounded soldiers, Bellavia reentered the building and fought insurgents single-handedly. With Regimental Combat Team 7's three assault battalions reaching Phase Line Fran ahead of schedule and securing Main Supply Route Michigan, Colonel Tucker shifted his logistics and line of communication to the main supply route.[186]

Company A, 1st Battalion, 8th Marines, began taking accurate sniper fire around 1400 hours from across Main Supply Route Michigan, while occupying the police building inside the government center. Meanwhile, at approximately 1430 hours, Company C, 1st Battalion, 8th Marines, began its assault from the al-Hadrah Mosque to seize the Imam al-Janabi's Saad Abi Bin Waqas Mosque (known as the "Blue" mosque for its prominent blue dome) about 1,000 meters east of the government center. However, as they moved out down Route Ethan, Company C, 1st Battalion, 8th Marines, came under sniper and machine-gun fire just 200 meters south. Some of that fire came from the same mosque minaret from which insurgents had earlier attacked Company B. Company C used close air support to destroy it.[187]

10 November:
General Natonski Revises His Assault Plan

By midday of 10 November, both of 1st Marine Division's assault regiments had secured their objectives at Phase Line Fran, which ran across central Fallujah. General Natonski wanted to press the attack and start an east-to-west assault through southern Fallujah. However, there were still pockets of resistance in the northeast of the city. Concerned about this, Regimental Combat Team 7 commanding officer Colonel Craig Tucker requested a delay crossing central Fallujah so that his three battalions could engage and clear the remaining insurgent threats. Concerned that such a move would slow 1st Marine Division's momentum, Natonski decided to call "an audible at the line of scrimmage" and revise his initial assault plan.

In the new plan, a battalion from each regiment would be held back to continue the clearing operations north of Phase Line Fran. The 3d Battalion, 5th Marines, would continue to clear the northwestern sector of Fallujah while 1st Battalion, 3d Marines, would finish clearing the northeast. Meanwhile, 3d Battalion, 1st Marines, and Task Force 2-7 would advance south and clear all areas west of Phase Line Henry while 1st Battalion, 8th Marines, and Task Force 2-2 would continue the attack south, east of the phase line. Natonski ordered the attack to begin at 1900 on 11 November.

During the evening of 10 November, 1st Battalion, 8th Marines' amphibious assault vehicles inserted Task Force High Value Target near the government center, about 100 meters west of the intersection of Phase Line Ethan and Fran, to provide overwatch for the battalion's Company C, 1st Battalion, 8th Marines' assault on Imam al-Janabi's Saad Abi Bin Waqas Mosque. Around 2200, Company C began clearing buildings around the mosque.[188] According to Captain Bethea, the tanks drew sniper fire during the company's movement to the al-Janabi Mosque. Second Platoon cleared the first row of homes to the west of the mosque, while 3d Platoon cleared the first row of homes to the north of the mosque and 1st Platoon cleared the row of homes north of 3d Platoon. The homes near the al-Janabi Mosque were large cement structures surrounded by cement walls and metal doors. The Marines used explosive breaches to enter almost every home. Once the built-up areas around the al-Janabi Mosque were secured, Captain Bethea directed the fire support team to co-locate with the force reconnaissance platoon on a rooftop across an open field located west of the al Janabi Mosque to overlook the mosque and the entire area surrounding it.

With Marines in place, Captain Bethea coordinated the assault on the mosque with the Iraqi Emergency Response Unit liaison officer and ordered the unit to move to the al-Janabi Mosque in amphibious assault vehicles. At 0300 hours on 11 November, the unit began its movement and subsequent attack to clear the al-Janabi Mosque.[189] Once Company C moved into support-by-fire positions around the mosque, amphibious assault vehi-

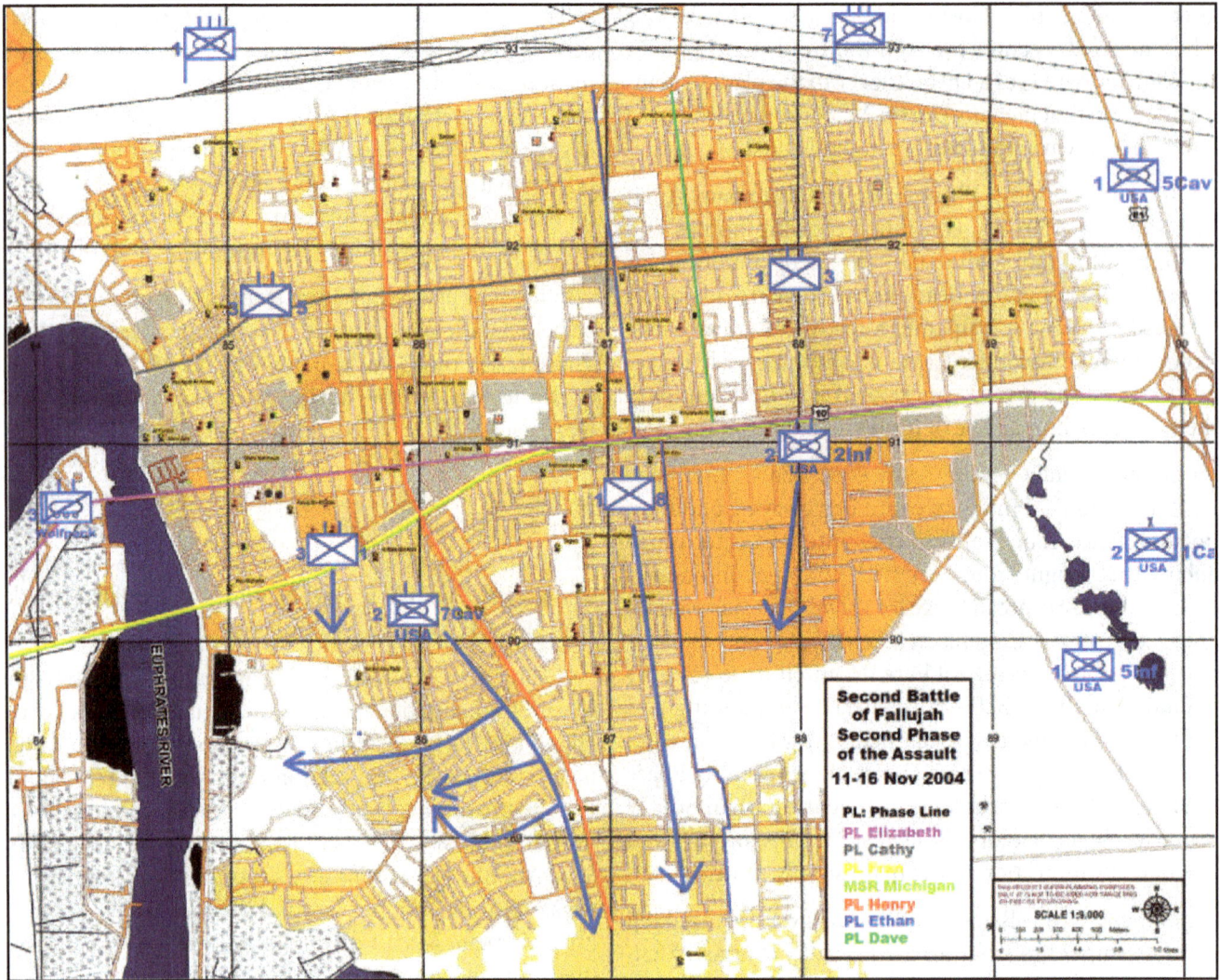

Second Battle
of Fallujah
Second Phase
of the Assault
11-16 Nov 2004

PL: Phase Line
PL Elizabeth
PL Cathy
PL Fran
MSR Michigan
PL Henry
PL Ethan
PL Dave

SCALE 1:9,000

Official U.S. Marine Corps map adapted by History Division

cles brought the Iraqi soldiers right up to the breach points that the tanks had created in the mosque walls in the early morning hours. Afterward, Bethea consolidated his forces. Meanwhile, Company B's Marines endured insurgent mortar fire during the night as they occupied the Iraqi National Guard compound.[190]

Meanwhile, outside Fallujah, insurgents began attacking the supply routes with IEDs and small-arms fire, including complex ambushes from insurgents hoping to fight their way into the city. At the same time, soldiers and Marines sealing the city also witnessed an increase in the number of civilians fleeing the fighting. However, U.S. forces allowed only women, children, and elderly to leave, forcing all military-age men to remain in the city.[191] On the western peninsula, Captain Conway's Company C, 3d Light Armored Reconnaissance Battalion, faced increased indirect fire on its checkpoints, and the high number of IEDs and ambushes on medical evacuation and resupply convoys forced Task Force Wolfpack to rely

entirely on Main Supply Route Michigan, Highway 10.[192] One such attack saw a vehicleborne IED destroy an ambulance, resulting in the severe wounding of the battalion surgeon, U.S. Navy Lieutenant Victor Lin, and several corpsmen. Insurgents similarly attacked Major Miller's Company B, 1st Battalion, 23d Marines' command posts. Company B, 1st Battalion, 23d Marines, and Company C, 3d Light Armored Reconnaissance Battalion, counterattacked known and suspected points of origin, and conducted simultaneous "cordon and knocks" that detained 11 insurgent suspects and resulted in decreased enemy attacks.[193]

Meanwhile, a Task Force Wolfpack convoy led by Captain Matthew T. Good suffered one killed and six wounded in action during a late night direct fire ambush where insurgents constructed a dirt berm across all four lanes of Main Supply Route Michigan and covered the obstacle with small-arms fire. Task Force Wolfpack responded with armor, rotary-wing, and fixed-wing close

Battle for Fallujah

air support.[194] By the end of the day, both of Major General Natonski's assault regiments had secured their initial objectives and had reached Phase Line Fran. Regimental Combat Team 1 had fought through the dense, hotly contested urban terrain of the Jolan District and reached Phase Line Fran after 43 hours of decisive operations, ahead of schedule.[195]

11 November: Advancing into Southern Fallujah

As dawn approached on 11 November 2004, the 1st Marine Division prepared for the second phase of the assault into Fallujah: crossing Highway 10 and clearing the city's southern districts. As the two regiments readied themselves for the attack across the central highway, they came under persistent sniper fire from insurgent forces. The insurgent attacks were coordinated and aggressive. The units based around the government center, 1st Battalion, 8th Marines, and Task Force High Value Target, in particular, came under determined sniper attack. Nevertheless, the Marine battalion maintained its efforts to prepare for its southern assault. East of 1st Battalion, 8th Marines' position, Task Force 2-2 turned over its sector north of Highway 10 to 1st Battalion, 3d Marines, around 0700 hours. Lieutenant Colonel Newell then prepared his battalion for a southwest attack along the city's edge to clear the foreign fighter stronghold of the industrial district.[196]

In Regimental Combat Team 1's sector, 3d Battalion, 1st Marines, reoriented itself to fight through Fallujah's southwest quadrant, an area that included the space between Phase Line Henry and the Euphrates River. Company K attacked down the western flank, Company I attacked down the center, and Company L attacked down the eastern flank along Phase Line Henry. As they reoriented themselves along Phase Line Elizabeth, the principal east-west line dividing the city, 1st Platoon, Company L, 3d Battalion, 1st Marines, uncovered yet more evidence of the intimidation that had been going on in Fallujah over the previous months. Inside the National Islamic Resistance Center, the Marines discovered blood on walls, bloodstained handprints, and blood-soaked sand used to clean the floor and the walls in the basement. The room also held a variety of videos. These included videos of beheadings, videos of attacks, and training videos providing instruction in the use of small arms, grenades, map reading, and range and direction finding for mortar and rocket employment. Finally, Marines found numerous computers, documents, and letters.

Photo by PFC Ralph Fabbri

The center of Regimental Combat Team 1's line was occupied by the 3d Battalion, 1st Marines, under the command of Col Willard A. Buhl (pictured here in 2009).

Moreover, 1st Platoon found the battle gear of Corporal Wassef Ali Hassoun. Corporal Hassoun, a Marine of Lebanese descent, had gone missing from his unit at Camp Fallujah during the previous summer and later turned up in Lebanon where he was returned to U.S. custody. The platoon also uncovered identification cards and other personal items as they swept captured buildings for intelligence. They also found further evidence that insurgents were using drugs to enhance their ability to continue fighting, finding syringes and vials of amphetamines and similar drugs. Outside the headquarters, Company L's Marines discovered an ice cream truck full of weapons and explosives used to make IEDs.[197]

As Company L, 3d Battalion, 1st Marines' first platoon established fighting positions on the rooftop of the Islamic Resistance headquarters, a large group of insurgents poured out of a mosque and attempted to envelop the platoon. Although 1st and 2d Platoons provided support by fire to 3d Platoon, they required artillery and close air support to defeat the insurgent counterattack.

Photo by SSgt Jonathan C. Knauth

Marines from Company B, 1st Battalion, 8th Marines, scale a wall on a rooftop between houses during the battle for Fallujah in November 2004.

The platoon suffered eight wounded and one killed in action. Later, Company L Marines encountered a number of insurgents believed to be on drugs, and a building rigged to explode. Just a few blocks away, Marines later discovered several weapons caches in the Fallujah Martyr's Cemetery.[198]

Meanwhile, 3d Battalion, 5th Marines, continued house-to-house clearing in the Jolan District. Companies K and L, 3d Battalion, 5th Marines, held on Phase Line Cathy as Company I fought through heavy insurgent fire to expand the battalion's boundary area of control. As Company I went house-to-house, Marines found a large weapons cache with more than 100 AK47s, 40 rocket-propelled grenades, and a variety of other weapons. Similarly, Company L also found a variety of weapons and munitions during their own searches. Captain Bitanga later recalled, "We found everything from TOW [tube-launched, optically tracked, wire-guided] missiles to homemade pistols made of pipe, rubber bands, and a nail.[199, 200]

As Company K searched buildings, it detained a large number of military-age males, and then found multiple weapons caches and what appeared to be an execution and torture chamber in the police captain's upscale neighborhood home. Company commander Captain McNulty recalled,

> It literally looked like something out of *Silence of the Lambs*, and you opened the door and behind the door there were two execution chambers built with their own head facilities, which is very unusual. There's typically only one or two per house.[201]

According to Major Bourgeois, the home was

> . . . a normal looking home until you opened up one door, and there were three cells in there; actual metal cells, with dirt floors, and there was one freshly killed individual in the first cell, bullet wound to his face—or to his head, and fresh blood in there. His feet were cut off. And then you went into another one, and there were actually two living individuals who were extremely emaciated and they looked to be—I don't want to say retarded, but they were malnourished to the

Battle for Fallujah

point where it affected their brain activity, because they were just acting strange. And then, in the farthest cell, which we didn't unlock, there was another individual who was apparently shot, because he was laying face down.[202]

During the afternoon of 11 November, 3d Battalion, 1st Marines, continued attacking through the al-Andalus District to Highway 10. Company L engaged in heavy fighting along Phase Line Henry and suffered another day of heavy casualties. As a result, the company remained in reserve at Highway 10, continuing to clear and block insurgents retreating north, while Companies I and K continued fighting south. In one action, Company K's Marines killed four insurgents and then came across the body of an insurgent in a nearby room. In fact, the insurgent had been faking death, and when the Marines entered he sprung up and attempted to kill them. Lance Corporal Justin D. McLeese killed the insurgent with his shotgun before he was fatally wounded by an improvised explosive.[203]

Meanwhile, in Regimental Combat Team 7's sector, Company C, 1st Battalion, 8th Marines, and Task Force High Value Target moved to the government center for re-tasking in amphibious tracked vehicles because of the continuous sniper activity.[204] "As soon as we got off the tracs," First Lieutenant Conner recalled, "everybody was saying like, 'Run! Get out of the open! There's snipers everywhere!' And sure enough, you know, you heard the bullets zinging by."[205] Lieutenant Colonel Brandl replaced Company A with Company C at the government center so that Companies A and B could continue advancing south. Meanwhile, 3d Battalion, 1st Marines' forward observers and forward air controllers used indirect fires and air attacks against insurgents in their path.[206] As the 1st Battalion, 8th Marines, began its assault across Main Supply Route Michigan (Highway 10) at 1400, one of the battalion's platoons was still engaged in a firefight that had begun that morning.

The first platoon of Company A, commanded by Second Lieutenant Elliot L. Ackerman, had seized a foothold just across Highway 10 that afforded good fields of fire the previous night (nicknamed the "candy store" by Marines). When the sun came up, the platoon surprised a group of insurgents walking down the street. However, insurgents reacted to 1st Platoon's attack by surrounding the "store," and two Marines would be injured in the ensuing firefight. Ackerman's Marines were still heavily engaged at the "candy store" around 1400 hours when 1st Battalion, 8th Marines, began its assault across Main Supply Route Michigan. Ordered by Captain Aaron Cun-

ningham to rejoin the company and protect its flank, the platoon was able to extricate itself from the firefight by blowing a hole through the "candy store" wall, escape insurgent fire, and fight through a narrow road to Company A's main body.[207]

Company A, 1st Battalion, 8th Marines, attacked south down Phase Line Frank with tanks and amphibious vehicles as Company B attacked southward down Phase Line Ethan from the Iraqi National Guard complex.[208] The battalion faced heavy resistance from determined foreign fighters: "There were enemy from the west, from the east, from the north," battalion commander Lieutenant Colonel Brandl recalled. "We were basically fighting a 360-degree fight."[209] Company A encountered heavy rocket-propelled grenade fire as it entered an alley nicknamed "hadji alley." "The moment we got into the alleyway though," First Lieutenant John Flanagan, Company A's Arab linguist and air intelligence officer, recalled, "we took pretty heavy fire and I think the lead tank took three rocket-propelled grenade shots within the first 200 meters, which didn't cause significant damage."[210] Meanwhile, Task Force 2-2 attacked through the industrial district along the city's edge, where Lieutenant Colonel Newell's soldiers discovered IED and vehicleborne IED factories, along with insurgent classrooms and spider holes where insurgents lived.[211]

With 1st Battalion, 8th Marines, attacking across Phase Line Fran into the Jubayl District, 1st Battalion, 3d Marines, began to expand its tactical area of responsibility. As the members of the battalion did, they encountered insurgents that had re-infiltrated the area after 1st Battalion, 8th Marines' rapid assault.[212] Lieutenant Colonel Ramos' Marines also discovered civilians for the first time. "It turned out that I didn't see anybody for the first 48 hours that we were in the city." Captain Tennant recalled, "I saw plenty of insurgents shooting at us and then I saw one family, about two days after we were in the city."[213]

During the day of 11 November, Colonel John R. Ballard, commanding officer of 4th Civil Affairs Group, accompanied General Natonski into Fallujah. General Natonski told Colonel Ballard that he wanted the civil-military operations center set up in the government center by the next day. In addition to providing humanitarian aid and restoring the city's essential services before civilians could come back into the city after the battle, one of the most pressing issues civil affairs Marines faced was removing the standing water that covered miles of the city's streets. With its pump stations inoperable, the city, which sat below the Euphrates, lacked the means of expelling the river's water. While the flooding caused little problem for

Photo by LCpl Ryan B. Busse

Vital close air support was provided throughout Operation al-Fajr by AH-1W Super Cobras from the 3d Marine Aircraft Wing.

tanks and amphibious vehicles, heavy engineer equipment such as the D9 bulldozers often got stuck. Moreover, the water also covered bodies and unexploded ordnance.[214]

On Fallujah's western border, Task Force Wolfpack fought through two direct fire ambushes as it attacked south to reopen and secure the lines of communication running from the west. Captain Conway's Marines, suffering several casualties, found 18 IEDs in a three-kilometer stretch of road. Insurgents unable to join their brethren in the city attacked Marines with ambushes and IEDs. Around 1545 hours, insurgents shot down a Super Cobra from Marine Light Attack Helicopter Squadron 169. Soldiers from Company C, 1st Battalion, 9th Infantry, commanded by Captain Victor A. Pirak, USA, along with elements of 3d Light Armored Reconnaissance Battalion's Headquarters and Service Company rescued and evacuated the wounded pilots. Insurgents with anti-aircraft weapons also shot down a second Bell AH-1W Super Cobra and damaged four U.S. Army Apache attack helicopters flying around Fallujah. The attacks resulted in no fatalities.

The Iraqi interim minister of health flew to the Fallujah hospital with a team of dignitaries and conducted a hos-

pital tour. As they visited, however, the hospital received indirect rocket fire. The attack wounded Task Force Wolfpack's executive officer, Major Kassner.[215]

During the evening of 11 November, in Regimental Combat Team 1's sector, 3d Battalion, 1st Marines, reached Phase Line Grace and stopped their attack for the rest of the night while U.S. Air Force Spectre gunships watched the city from above and continued engaging insurgents. Company K seized the Resala District flour factory on Phase Line Grace, then held its positions for the night to rest and refit for the next day's assault. At around 1900 hours, Task Force 2-7, which had spent the day rearming, refitting, and refueling, launched its attack into southern Fallujah along Phase Line Henry. Company C, 3d Battalion, 8th Cavalry, led the assault without the cover of infantry because the streets in the southern quarter of the city were too narrow for 3d Battalion, 1st Marines, to accompany Task Force 2-7's tanks and Bradleys. As a result, 3d Battalion, 1st Marines, had to wait for the soldiers to advance down Phase Line Henry and then shift laterally down the side streets.

Company A, 2d Battalion, 7th Cavalry, followed Company C, 3d Battalion, 8th Cavalry, down Phase Line

Battle for Fallujah

Henry to ensure they did not get cut off by maneuvering bands of insurgents, encountering only minimal resistance.[216] The company attacked with a tank platoon on each flank and an infantry platoon in the center.[217] Captain Glass recalled, "Obviously, it took a little bit of time to maneuver through the narrow streets, and sometimes we couldn't find how to get through because the road wasn't clear enough, so we would have to back up and find another way through."[218] Captain Glass' soldiers reached the southern limits of the city before dawn where they set up a defense. Company A, 2d Battalion, 7th Cavalry, attacked behind them, encountering heavy resistance and formed a picket line along Phase Line Henry to support 3d Battalion, 1st Marines' attack.[219] However, during the assault, Task Force 2-7 ran short on ammunition, especially 120mm mortars. Unable to receive these particular rounds from the supporting Marine infantry, the ammunition was air supplied by the 2d Battalion, 227th Aviation Regiment, in dense fog and low visibility.[220]

In Fallujah's east, Task Force 2-2 had to halt its attack around 2000 hours so that 1st Battalion, 8th Marines, could catch up to protect its flank and elements of the 2d Brigade Combat Team (2d Brigade, 1st Cavalry Division), could move out of the way of Task Force 2-2's fires. The task force resumed its assault at 2300. At the same time, Companies A and B, 1st Battalion, 8th Marines, fought into the night, clearing house-to-house as tanks and amphibious assault vehicles provided support. Brandl's Marines attacked insurgent strongholds supported by AC-130 gunships and F/A-18 Hornet attack aircraft. After fighting approximately 1,000 meters into Fallujah's southern district, 1st Battalion, 8th Marines, ended its attack for the night to prepare for the next day.[221]

12 November:
Continued Advances into Southern Fallujah

In southwest Fallujah, Task Force 2-2 attacked through the Sinah or "industrial district" through the night until about 0530 hours on 12 November when it hit Phase Line Isabel, one of the roads forming the southern boundaries of the city. Task Force 2-2 found itself in the middle of a complex ambush as teams of insurgents attacked the soldiers from various directions.[222] According to Lieutenant Colonel Newell, "As the sun came up, all these guys came out of their holes and started shooting rocket-propelled grenades."[223] During the engagement, U.S. Army First Lieutenant Edward D. Iwan, Company A, 2d Battalion, 2d Infantry's executive officer, was killed by rocket-propelled grenade fire. Because insurgents had come between Task Force 2-2's main force and the supporting

Photo by SPC Chastity R. Boykin, USA

Task Force 2-7, an Army task force, gave Regimental Combat Team 1 an armored spearhead for its advance into western Fallujah. The unit was led by LtCol James E. Rainey (photographed here as a colonel in 2010).

Iraqi forces, Newell made the decision to back up, reorganize, and wait for 1st Battalion, 8th Marines, to catch up and protect the flank. Newell wanted to press the attack to prevent the "very well-trained" foreign fighters from regrouping.[224]

West of Newell's soldiers, Company A, 1st Battalion, 8th Marines, and Company B, 1st Battalion, 8th Marines, resumed their advance at 0300 hours, moving south and then west, successfully seizing a mosque west of Phase Line Ethan. During the attack, Company B's 1st Platoon suffered seven casualties after engaging insurgents hiding in a building near the mosque. Before dawn, Companies A and B had attacked about 800 meters south of Task Force High Value Target's positions. As the sun came up, Task Force High Value Target observed large groups of insurgents coming out of the buildings and preparing to attack 1st Battalion, 8th Marines, from behind. Task Force High Value Target engaged the insurgents with snipers and machine guns for several hours, exposing their positions, while calling in with artillery and close air support. About 0900 hours, insurgents surrounded the mosque and attacked Company B, beginning a 12-hour firefight.[225]

Task Force High Value Target began receiving rocket-propelled grenade fire from the mosque next door, injuring Team 3's Marines. Although they had cleared the building the previous night, insurgents had reentered the buildings to fire on the government center. About that time, the reconnaissance Marines took heavy caliber fire that they believed was from a friendly .50-caliber weapon, injuring a Marine.[226] With the Marines unable to call in

Soldiers from Task Force 2-7 load a mortar round during Operation al-Fajr on 12 November 2004.

close air support due to the close-quarters nature of the fight, Lieutenant Colonel Brandl sent an amphibious assault vehicle to extract Task Force High Value Target.[227]

In Fallujah's south, half of Company C, 3d Battalion, 8th Cavalry, had returned to the train station to refuel and rearm, including Captain Glass, which left Captain Twaddell in charge of Company A, 2d Battalion, 7th Cavalry, and half of Company C, 3d Battalion, 8th Cavalry. Both companies were arrayed along Phase Line Henry, with either a section of tanks or Bradleys on each major intersection. "We moved through the night, bounding one Phase Line ahead at a time with minimal contact." Captain Twaddell recalled, "We were all incredibly tired and staying alert was difficult. . . . As the sun came up, the enemy came out to fight. We began taking intense mortar and rocket-propelled grenade fire."[228] Captain Twaddell consolidated both companies to get out of the way of an air strike on insurgent positions ahead.

Around 0900 hours, insurgent mortar fire intensified as Task Force 2-7 was still waiting for the air strike. "I made the decision right there," Captain Twaddell recalled, "to maneuver this company—plus on the enemy rather than sit there and take mortar fire."[229] Twaddell extended

his tanks and Bradleys along Phase Line Isabel and attacked south. During the engagement, insurgents scored considerable damage to Task Force 2-7's Bradleys, injuring several soldiers. Captain Twaddell's Bradley was hit with an RPG, killing an interpreter and injuring three soldiers. After the engagement, Captain Chris Brooke's Company C, 2d Battalion, 7th Cavalry, came in to support while Company A refitted.[230]

Meanwhile, 3d Battalion, 1st Marines, began its assault into the Nazal District, nicknamed "Queens" for its dense, poorer neighborhoods. Company I, 3d Battalion, 1st Marines, advanced on the battalion's right while Company K moved on the left, along Phase Line Henry, clearing side streets as they moved south. Because of the heavy casualties suffered during the first three days of combat, Company L remained in reserve holding the key intersection at the center of the city. From there, the company conducted operations to clear those areas behind the line of advance still occupied by insurgent forces. Lieutenant Colonel Buhl's battalion was supposed to have begun its attack at 0500 hours, but the lead company, Company K, was delayed because it was taking mortar fire coming from a mosque on Phase Line Henry. At the same time, Buhl's Marines came under heavy insurgent sniper fire

Battle for Fallujah

Photo by SSgt Jonathan C. Knauth

Marines from Company B, 1st Battalion, 8th Marines, travel aboard an amphibious assault vehicle along a street in Fallujah in late November.

from Regimental Combat Team 7's sector. Only after one of Task Force 2-7's Bradleys finally destroyed the insurgents' positions at the mosque and Captain Bodisch's tank neutralized the snipers could 3d Battalion, 1st Marines, commence its attack.

Company K encountered heavy resistance at the central intersection of Phase Lines Henry and Fran where insurgents had placed several IEDs and registered it for indirect fire. After taking several casualties, Company K then fought a running battle in the rain along Highway 10, which was lined with IEDs. As they moved, the company took intense small-arms, rocket-propelled grenade, and mortar fire.[231] Lance Corporal Boswood recalled,

> So, the whole company spread out, punched way out to the sides of the road, and just started pushing, and it was nothing but a gun battle the whole way down. It was intense firing coming from everybody in the company, all the way down the road; from machine-gunners mowing down 12 to 15 guys in one alleyway, to that lone rifleman up front, just popping 'em off one at a time, it went all the way down the road, all day long.[232]

Company I also fought a running battle down an IED-laden street, codenamed Phase Line Isaac. The rifle company also encountered insurgents who fell back but did not surrender. Insurgent units ranged from three-to-four man teams to squad-size formations. They fought a running battle with scattered bands of insurgents who fired on Marines, dropped their weapons, and fell back to the next weapons cache.[233] By moving through the city unarmed, the insurgents could then masquerade as non-combatants. "That way they didn't have to travel with the weapons, probably hoping to use our ROE [rules of engagement] against us," Captain Jeffrey S. McCormack, 3d Battalion, 1st Marines' intelligence officer, described.[234] Near the "Green" Mosque for example, First Lieutenant Michael S. Deland's Marines encountered an insurgent pretending to be dead, who then detonated a grenade that wounded two Marines.[235]

In northwest Fallujah, Colonel Shupp turned security of the Jolan District to Iraqi forces and ordered 3d Battalion, 5th Marines, to move south to support 3d Battalion, 1st Marines, as they attacked south.[236] The battalion encountered fiercer resistance from a large number of more fanatical, better equipped, and better trained foreign fighters, some speaking Chechen, with light skin and red hair. The 3d Battalion, 1st Marines, pushed insurgents south, hoping to trap them into an area where they could not escape. However, insurgents managed to escape through holes in walls and into shallow tunnels through spider holes dug into building floors. Other insurgents did not flee when Marines approached, however, but instead waited to ambush them entering the buildings. To counter this threat, Marines would fall back from the building and call in a bulldozer.

The 1st Battalion, 8th Marines, advanced much farther south than 3d Battalion, 1st Marines. This created problems coordinating fires across the boundary between the two battalions and also allowed insurgents to move across unchallenged.[237] Company A, 1st Battalion, 8th Marines, held its position for much of the day as Company B fought insurgents at the mosque with the support of Spectre gunships that pounded insurgent positions with accurate and deadly 105mm artillery. Around 1500 hours, Company A began moving south again, advancing rapidly toward Phase Line Isabel at the city's southern limits.[238] Around 1630 hours, Company C began simultaneous clearing operations along the northern, western, and southern sectors of the government center, two rows of buildings on each of those sides, to create a buffer zone around the compound.[239] The company then established defense-in-depth outside of the compound. Around 1700 hours, Company B left the mosque and fought down Phase Line Ethan to keep up with Company A and reach Phase Line Isabel.[240]

In northeast Fallujah, Regimental Combat Team 7 began providing humanitarian aid at the al-Hadrah Mosque to the civilians who were either too elderly or sick to evacuate, held hostage by insurgent groups, or stayed in the city to safeguard their property and interests. Not far away, 1st Battalion, 3d Marines, breached homes and courtyards and fought close-quarters engagements as they cleared homes with insurgents waiting in ambush with Russian RPK light machine guns using armor-piercing rounds pointed through holes in walls. At the government center, civil affairs teams moved in and began establishing the civil-military operations center 200 meters away from Colonel Michael A. Shupp's Regimental Combat Team 1 headquarters.[241]

In southwest Fallujah, Company I and Company K, 3d Battalion, 1st Marines, had fought hard and fast through the Resala District and reached Phase Line Isabel on the city's edge around 1800 hours. Company K suffered 1 killed and 20 wounded in action.[242] Meanwhile, as Task Force 2-7 held its position along Phase Line Henry in support of 3d Battalion, 1st Marines, Lieutenant Colonel Rainey's soldiers came under attack from multiple groups of insurgents throughout the day, prompting him to bring in Company A, 2d Battalion, 7th Cavalry.[243] "We started encountering more and more professional insurgents," Major Karcher recalled. "There were reports of guys maneuvering wearing body armor and Kevlar helmets, which they likely stole from the Iraqi National Guard."[244]

In southeast Fallujah, Task Force 2-2's assault companies had switched positions during the day for a renewed attack to Fallujah's southern edge. As night fell on the city, the armored task force resumed its advance through the industrial area. As the soldiers cleared the industrial district, they killed several insurgents and found numerous weapons caches. In one location on the south side of the industrial sector, soldiers found 20 enemy dead by an abandoned truck repair shop; they had been lined up and shot with single bullet to the head. Newell's soldiers also discovered an extensive underground tunnel network that allowed insurgents to escape down spider holes and reemerge somewhere else soldiers and Marines had already cleared. In these tunnels, soldiers found dead foreign fighters and foreign passports. By midnight, Task Force 2-2 had assaulted 1,000 meters past Phase Line Isabel before it stood down for the night.[245]

Meanwhile, 1st Battalion, 8th Marines, attacked into the night to catch up with Task Force 2-2 and reached Phase Line Isabel around 2300 hours. During their assault, Marines found that insurgents had rigged some buildings to explode. Both companies discovered weapons caches and surrendering insurgents. Poring through the documents found on dead insurgents and in their hideouts, the Marines found evidence of foreign fighters coming from Syria, Sudan, Jordan, and Afghanistan, along with Chechens, Palestinians, and Iranians. As Lieutenant Colonel Brandl's battalion attacked into the night, aircraft flying overhead provided intelligence, surveillance, and reconnaissance using thermal imagery, which allowed the battalion to identify and engage insurgents hiding in homes. As the battalion moved south, however, it moved closer to Regimental Combat Team 1 on the west and Task Force 2-2 on the east, limiting the scope of fires the battalion could put down.[246]

By the end of 12 November, Regimental Combat Teams 1 and 7 had reached Fallujah's southern limits. After five days of sustained fighting, soldiers and Marines had pushed through Fallujah and secured all of their objectives. Major Stephen J. Winslow, a field historian, noted in his personal account, "The Marines and soldiers are extremely tired. They are extremely dirty."[247]

Photo by LCpl James J. Vooris

A Marine from Company L, 3d Battalion, 5th Marines, readies his M4 carbine while manning a rooftop in Fallujah on 15 November 2004.

13 November: Redeployment, Consolidation, and the Fight at the House of Hell

On 13 November, with the initial objectives of Operation al-Fajr achieved, the 1st Marine Division's planners divided the city into sectors and began the detailed, methodical clearing of the city to kill insurgents and destroy weapons caches found during the initial assault.[248] Each battalion rotated Marines into and out of the fight so that they could rest. While many insurgents, willing to die for their cause, waited inside buildings to ambush Marines and soldiers, other insurgents saw the hopelessness of their effort and surrendered:

> We gave them [insurgents] no rest, recalled Major Lawrence K. Hussey, Regimental Combat Team 7's intelligence officer, and when we finally got into the fifth and sixth day . . . they're coming out of nowhere, waving white flags. . . . they're worn out . . . [and] there have been places where we've gone in—8, 10, 11, 14 guys inside a house,

and they would just give up as soon as guys came in, or as soon as they saw units approaching . . .[249]

However, many of these insurgents used the white flag as a decoy and struck at Marines as soon they were close.[250]

In southwest Fallujah, 3d Battalion, 1st Marines, established bases and began clearing their sectors while Task Force 2-7 continued to hold on Phase Line Henry in support.[251] The 4th Battalion, 1st Iraqi Intervention Force, moved into southwest Fallujah to support 3d Battalion, 1st Marines.[252] Company I, 3d Battalion, 1st Marines, moved north to Phase Line Fran and began detailed clearing of the area the battalion had swept quickly through the day before alongside Company L.

Meanwhile, Company K, 3d Battalion, 1st Marines, began clearing around their base in southern Fallujah.[253] Soon after Company K began clearing houses in their sector, a squad from 3d Platoon entered a large two-story building and was caught in an ambush, leaving several wounded Marines trapped inside with several well-armed foreign insurgents in fortified positions willing to fight to the death.[254]

Photo by SFC Johan Charles Van Boers, USA

Fallujah was known as the "City of Mosques" and the hundreds of mosques in the city dominated the skyline. HMMWVs from Task Force 2-7 pass one of the mosques as they patrol the streets of the city on 21 November 2004.

With injured Marines trapped in the building, Corporal Robert J. Mitchell Jr.'s squad came to assist and was joined by First Sergeant Bradley A. Kasal, from the battalion's Weapons Company. Mitchell's squad charged the building and took up firing positions as insurgents fired down on Marines from a catwalk, wounding Kasal and three other Marines who became trapped in the building. The structure was later dubbed "House of Hell." For three hours, Marines tried to breach the barred windows, walls, and locked doors until finally penetrating the building and extracting the wounded Marines under fire, and then destroyed the house with a 20-pound satchel charge.[255] "Tremendous explosion," First Lieutenant Jacobs recalled.

> House comes down. Completely rubbled the house. We go to survey the damage to see if we can find any of the enemy KIA [killed in action]. We look around on one side of the house, we don't find anything. We assume everybody's dead. So, we start to make our way back to the firm base. As we're walking past the house, a hand comes up out of the rubble, throws a hand grenade at us.

Everybody saw the grenade coming, so we were able to scatter. The grenade goes off. The Marines were pretty much in a school circle around the guy, and just unleashed hell on 'em. Must've shot him about 100 times.[256]

Marines attributed the insurgents' apparent "superhuman abilities" to the use of adrenaline and other drugs, such as cocaine, heroin, and methamphetamines, because soldiers and Marines discovered these during their searches.[257] Captain McCormack noted that chest rigs were all standardized, indicating a certain degree of professionalism, with magazine pouches across their chest, a stash of U.S. and Iraqi money on one side, and a stash of opium on the other. Company K suffered 10 friendly wounded in action and 1 killed in action during the engagement.[258] Kasal and Corporal Mitchell each received the Navy Cross for their actions during the fight.

Meanwhile, Company I, 3d Battalion, 1st Marines, moved east to west toward the Euphrates River, moving through the same neighborhoods the battalion had traversed during the initial assault. In one action, Lance

Battle for Fallujah

Photo by SSgt Jonathan C. Knauth

Clearing Fallujah's many houses and other buildings was exceptionally dangerous work. Insurgents would stage ambushes from the second story of buildings, attacking Marines in the stairwells with grenades and automatic fire. In this image, Marines from 1st Battalion, 8th Marines, prepare to clear a house suspected of containing insurgent forces.

Corporal McLeese died entering a house that insurgents rigged with an IED, also injuring some of his fellow Marines. In another action, Company I Marines assaulted the green mosque, which Company K had cleared the day before, and discovered that insurgents had re-infiltrated the mosque and again used it to attack Marines. After the engagement, Company I's Marines cautiously entered the mosque and found dead and wounded insurgents inside. One Marine saw an insurgent move and quickly shot him, believing that like the previous day he was only playing dead and would attack them. Journalist Kevin Sites, who had joined Company I as it entered the building, recorded the event with his video camera. Without knowing what had transpired, and apparently unaware of insurgents playing dead and then attacking soldiers and Marines, websites reported the incident to Marine officials, and waited 18 hours before sharing the footage with the media pool so that the Marines could review it and conduct an investigation.[259]

As 3d Battalion, 1st Marines, cleared the "Queens" District of southwest Fallujah, Task Force 2-7 continued taking fire along Phase Line Henry for the second day. Around 1130, 1st Platoon, Company A, 2d Battalion, 7th Cavalry, came in contact with insurgents firing from buildings. Soldiers chased an insurgent across an alley and into a building where 10–20 insurgents were waiting in ambush inside. The ensuing engagement resulted in several injuries and the death of U.S. Army Specialist Jose A. Velez.[260]

At this point, when Marines and soldiers encountered insurgents in buildings, they backed off and attacked them with tanks and bulldozers. Major General Natonski recalled the challenges of limiting damage to the city while also trying to clear it of insurgent forces:

> We wanted to minimize, as much as we could, the damage to the city, so that if we were attacked by small arms we would return fire with small arms or a step above. However, I will tell you as the battle went on, and there are a lot of people that will tell you firsthand, when it came to deciding

November - December 2004

whether we were going to put a Marine or soldier's life on the line it was a lot easier to take the building down with a bomb, a bulldozer, a tank, or explosives. And we would have rather done that than put a Marine's or soldier's life on the line.[261]

On numerous occasions, the Marines and soldiers of the 1st Marine Division confronted the danger of insurgents using presumably cleared buildings to stage ambushes. At around 1400, as the companies of Task Force 2-2 prepared to continue their advance into the industrial district, U.S. Army Captain Sean P. Sims, Company A, 2d Battalion, 2d Infantry's commanding officer, went into a building he believed had been cleared hoping to view the city from the top of the building and plan his attack. Inside the building, however, insurgents waited in ambush and killed Captain Sims. The company's first sergeant, Peter L. Smith, USA, took command and finished preparing the company for the attack.[262]

As Task Force 2-2 planned its attack, Company A and Company B, 1st Battalion, 8th Marines, established bases along Phase Line Isabel, and then began to search buildings. As they did, they found numerous weapons caches and captured some insurgents. Lieutenant Colonel Brandl's Marines would spend some of the day preparing for the final assault south from Phase Line Isabel to Phase Line Jenna, the southern border of the city. At 1200 hours on 13 November, Major Mark E. Winn, the 1st Battalion, 8th Marines' executive officer, tasked Captain Bethea's Company C with seizing the mosque across from Fallujah's government center and two multilevel buildings west of the mosque that Task Force High Value Target had vacated the previous morning. Captain Bethea quickly developed a scheme of maneuver and then briefed his company's key leaders and the fire support team on his plan, purpose, and end state. Company C's Weapons Platoon would remain at the government center while the rest of the company attacked the new objectives.[263]

At 1345, Major General Natonski, Colonel Tucker, and Lieutenant Colonel Brandl arrived to observe Company C's attack. At 1415, Mobile Assault Platoon 3 engaged the objectives with tube-launched, optically tracked, wire-guided (TOW) missiles, .50 caliber machine guns, and MK19 40mm automatic grenade launchers. Second Lieutenant Turner's 2d Platoon then attacked the multilevel building west of the mosque with Captain Bethea, First Sergeant Andrade, and First Lieutenant Miller, and headquarters Marines co-located with the platoon, and 3d Platoon attacked the multilevel building east of the mosque. As Captain Bethea's Marines attacked the new objectives, a group of insurgents maneuvered toward the govern-

ment center from the northwest, answering a call-to-battle broadcast from an area mosque's loud speakers. As they did, a Navy SEAL team and supporting Marines engaged the enemy moving toward them and killed 22 insurgents.[264] By 1730, Company C secured all objectives.[265]

Meanwhile, the 3d Battalion, 5th Marines, and 1st Battalion, 3d Marines, continued to clear and secure northern Fallujah's districts. In the course of the fight, Marines and soldiers continued to see evidence of the type of regiment that had controlled Fallujah during the previous months. At one point, Company L, 3d Battalion, 5th Marines, discovered another execution and the body of a blonde woman on the street with her face slashed open and her legs, arms, and breasts cut off.[266] The U.S. forces also continued to face the problem of whether to seize centers of resistance or use close air support to destroy buildings suspected of being insurgent bases. At one point Company K, 3d Battalion, 5th Marines, took sniper fire from one building that detainees stated housed a large insurgent force. Captain McNulty decided to call in close air support and the building was ultimately destroyed by five 500-pound bombs. Nevertheless, it was later shown that the detainees' reports were incorrect.[267]

The Marines of 1st Battalion, 3d Marines, clearing Fallujah's northeast, encountered numerous insurgent ambushes that further explain McNulty's concerns, however. In one action, Marines from Company C's 1st Platoon breached the door of a building and encountered insurgents waiting in ambush. Two of the Marines stacked outside the door got in the building quickly as the rest of their squad waited outside for them to clear the first room before they rushed inside. Insurgents started throwing hand grenades down from the second deck and wounded 10 Marines from the platoon right outside the building, and as the Marines started to fall back to get behind some cover, some were shot. However, the insurgents did not know that Lance Corporal Buck M. Gates and Lance Corporal Fahiye A. Yusuf were inside the building because they had gotten in so quickly. When four insurgents ran down the stairs toward them, Gates and Yusuf killed them and left the building with at least four other insurgents trapped inside. The entrapped fighters continued to fire small-arms fire and rocket-propelled grenades throughout the night, at one point injuring Marines in another building. After Company C fired an antitank weapon into the building, the incoming fire stopped. "We found 11 dead insurgents inside that house," Captain Tennant recalled.

That was the largest single pocket of resistance that we had encountered and I think the largest that we did the entire time, one place at one time. And

Battle for Fallujah

Marines from 3d Battalion, 1st Marines, climb through rubble as they advance into a structure during the battalion's advance into south Fallujah.

we searched those guys and found that they had Syrian, Jordanian, Saudi Arabian passports. Each one of them had a crisp, brand new American one hundred dollar bill. We later learned that many of the insurgents had been promised one thousand dollars if they fought the Americans. They would get one hundred dollars up front and the other nine hundred once the Americans had been chased away from the city. Obviously, it didn't work out too good for them. So we medevaced [medical evacuation] I guess 11 Marines that day. We killed 11 insurgents, but medevaced 11.[268]

During the afternoon in southwest Fallujah, 3d Battalion, 1st Marines, endured bitter fighting as it continued clearing the Resala District. In the southeast, Task Force 2-2 attacked south on schedule through the industrial district at 1400 and reached the southern side of the city within an hour. Meanwhile, 1st Battalion, 8th Marines, continued searching buildings along Phase Line Isabel. At approximately 1615, Task Force 2-2 moved to a logistics supply point near the cloverleaf to rearm and refuel.

At 1725, the armored task force returned to southern Fallujah, moved west across 1st Battalion, 8th Marines' position, and then turned south to resume its attack at 1745.

Meanwhile Lieutenant Colonel Brandl's 1st Battalion, 8th Marines, prepared for the next day's assault. Company B, 1st Battalion, 8th Marines, moved up across an open field to gain better observation and fields of fire in preparation for the next day's attack. After crossing the midpoint of an open field, the companies came under heavy small-arms fire, RPK, and machine-gun fire from the east along Phase Line Henry, forcing Marines into a 100-meter full sprint to reach the cover of a compound. Once across the field, they continued to receive small-arms and rocket-propelled grenade fire for the remainder of the day. As the companies rested, insurgent fire subsided as U.S. Air Force gunships came on station to attack insurgents through the night.[269]

In northern Fallujah, both 3d Battalion, 5th Marines, and 1st Battalion, 3d Marines, continued searching their sectors while Regimental Combat Team 7's humanitarian aid station at the al-Hadrah Mosque became a busy center as more civilians came for food and assistance. At this

Photo by LCpl James J. Vooris

A working dog handler and his K-9 partner assigned to Company L, 3d Battalion, 5th Marines, patrol an area of Fallujah during Operation al-Fajr.

point in the battle, after four full days of fighting, Marines began to conduct reconstruction and humanitarian operations in those areas cleared of insurgent forces.[270] On Fallujah's periphery, soldiers and Marines continued engaging insurgents trying to get into the city.[271]

At Fallujah's train station, Task Force 2-7's Lieutenant Colonel Rainey and his operations officer, Major Karcher, visited Lieutenant Colonel Buhl and his operations officer, Major Christeen Griffin, and proposed doing more to support 3d Battalion, 1st Marines' clearing efforts. With that, Lieutenant Colonel Buhl agreed to let Task Force 2-7's armor go in before his Marines.[272] In southwest Fallujah, Task Force 2-2 continued clearing the industrial area into the night. During Newell's attack, his brigade recon troop attacked "confused" groups of insurgents attempting to regroup while AC-130 gunships and armed General Atomics MQ-1 Predator unmanned aerial vehicles killed groups of insurgents attempting to maneuver. Not everything went well for Newell's soldiers, however. "The hard part about moving around in the dark," Newell recalled, "is that we eventually had two tanks fall essentially into collapsed tunnels and, in both cases, their front

ends are literally sticking straight up in the air. We finished the attack at 2200, but it takes us another three hours to extract the tanks from the battlefield."[273] Ultimately Colonel Newell's soldiers destroyed these insurgent bunkers and tunnels with artillery and air strikes. The air attacks included dropping four 2,000-pound bunker-busting bombs on a large underground complex.[274]

14–15 November: Continued Consolidation

Recognizing that insurgents fleeing Task Force 2-2's assault had fled across 1st Battalion, 8th Marines' zone of operations, the two assault regiments came together on the morning of 14 November and began a second effort to clear the southern areas of the city. Company C, 3d Battalion, 8th Cavalry, attacked in support of 3d Battalion, 1st Marines, drawing insurgent fire in advance of 3d Battalion, 1st Marines' attack. Company A, 2d Battalion, 7th Cavalry, pulled back to reserve, and Company C, 2d Battalion, 7th Cavalry, moved forward to hold Phase Line Henry from the city's southern boundary to Highway 10.[275]

Battle for Fallujah

In the east, Companies A and B, 1st Battalion, 8th Marines, were online with 3d Battalion, 1st Marines. Attacking quickly, Lieutenant Colonel Brandl's Marines did not have time to search every house. At one location, Company A, 1st Battalion, 8th Marines, discovered an IED-making factory, along with open food containers, cigarettes, load-bearing vests, identification cards, communication devices, and weapons that told Marines that insurgents had either left in a hurry or never returned. Marines also found 60mm mortar tubes and an abundance of enemy documents, many with al-Zarqawi's emblem.[276]

In the Jolan District, the civil affairs team supporting 3d Battalion, 5th Marines, initiated the first efforts to remove dead enemy fighters and provide them with a proper Muslim burial. Aware of Muslim traditions regarding the treatment of the dead, Captain Henry A. Henegar made arrangements to allow Iraqis from a nearby town to enter the city with two trucks and remove the bodies under the supervision of the civil affairs team. The Iraqis chanted prayers as they handled the dead.[277]

At about 1020, elements of 3d Platoon, Company K encountered insurgents immediately north of the Martyr's Cemetery where 3d Battalion, 1st Marines, had fought heavily three days before. While clearing buildings in the al-Andalus District, Lance Corporal George J. Payton led a team with bayonets attached through a doorway and was killed by insurgents. Company K then fought across a cemetery, defeating heavy machine-gun fire with machine guns and tanks before finally reaching Phase Line Fran. During the assault, Company K also discovered several weapons caches, including a command and control center, and Iraqi soldiers working with Task Force Bruno discovered an IED factory in the central Jolan District. Meanwhile, the battalion's Task Force Bruno had grown to 150 personnel, and continued to clear areas behind the battalion with Iraqi forces. That afternoon, around 1600, Lieutenant Colonel Malay reopened the Blackwater Bridge and crossed it with Major General Natonski and Colonel Shupp to meet Lieutenant Colonel Dinauer and his Task Force Wolfpack.[278]

Meanwhile, approximately 25 insurgents who had dug in on the western bank of the Euphrates River ambushed Major Wittnam's Small Craft Company. The company returned fire and dismounted to counterattack, killing seven insurgents. Meanwhile, U.S. Army AH-46 Apache attack helicopters continued receiving heavy surface-to-air, rocket-propelled grenade, and antiaircraft artillery fire while patrolling Fallujah's periphery. Apaches engaged and destroyed vehicles carrying insurgent rockets and

Photo by LCpl Daniel J. Klein

A member of the Iraqi National Guard attached to Regimental Combat Team 7 provides security for a humanitarian mission during the Second Battle of Fallujah. Iraqi soldiers formed an integral part of the 1st Marine Division during its assault on Fallujah in November, performing more capably than they had during the first battle for the city the previous spring.

mortars. In response to insurgent attacks in Mosul, the U.S. Army's 1st Battalion, 5th Infantry, left Fallujah's periphery to return to Mosul. Consequently Lieutenant Colonel Myles Miyamasu's 1st Battalion, 5th Cavalry, expanded its coverage by about 50 kilometers and assumed responsibility for al-Karmah, al-Anbar Province.[279]

By the morning of 15 November, Fallujah was noticeably quiet, although Marines and soldiers continued to use artillery and air strikes against insurgent positions.[280] In a press conference, Colonel Michael R. Regner, I Marine Expeditionary Force's operations officer, told reporters that Fallujah was "secure," explaining that Marines continued to clear the city of insurgents.[281] Regner's reports amplified Lieutenant General Sattler's comments the day before when he told reporters that "the city has been seized. We have liberated the city of al-Fallujah." Colonel Regner nevertheless cautioned that Marines and soldiers would continue to clear Fallujah "for at least four or five more days," although it would ultimately take another five weeks.[282] Marines estimated that about 1,200 insurgents were killed during combat operation, whereas U.S. casualties were 38 killed in action and 275 wounded in action, and 6 Iraqi soldiers killed.[283]

Meanwhile, after four days of clearing in southwest Fallujah, Company K, 3d Battalion, 1st Marines, received an order to move north while Company I continued advancing to Phase Line Jenna. Company L moved back to the train station to rest and refit for the day because of the disproportionate number of casualties it had sustained. The 3rd Battalion, 5th Marines, conducted a slight boundary shift and advanced from Highway 10 behind 3d Battalion, 1st Marines.[284] Before beginning its attack, however, Company K, 3d Battalion, 5th Marines, discovered six dead Iraqis in an alley. Major Bourgeois recalled,

> I got up at 0600, brushed my teeth on top of the roof looking at the sunrise, went to go spit my toothpaste over the side of the building, and I see six Iraqi bodies just laying in the courtyard next to me just all blown to heck. Their bodies were intact, so we assumed that they were executed, but actually one of the Shehwanis [General Mohammed Abdullah Mohammed Shehwani's 1st Iraqi Inter-vention Force Brigade] went by and checked, and he said some of their throats had been cut.[285]

Later, Marines found six more dead Iraqis, which Major Bourgeois described as "piled like cord wood that had been dead obviously a while; the stench was just horrendous. Maggots all throughout their faces and stuff. So, that would indicate that they'd been there a little while."[286] By the end of the day, 3d Battalion, 5th Marines, reached Phase Line Grace, the limits of its clearing operations.[287]

In southeast Fallujah, Task Force 2-2 began a deliberate effort to clear every structure along the line of advance in dismounted fashion after resting and refitting the previous day. "We went back up and we just did it again," recalled Newell, "although the contact on the 15th and 16th was negligible . . . and [we] opened up every single garage and building."[288] During the clearing, Company A, 2d Battalion, 2d Infantry, found numerous weapons caches and captured a group of insurgents. Captain Walter described the prisoners as "a lot of military-aged men with recently shaved beards, one of them with a gunshot wound to his leg being pushed in a wheelchair."[289]

Meanwhile, 1st Battalion, 8th Marines, moved past Phase Line Jenna to the desert beyond Fallujah's southern limits.[290] Advancing beyond the city's boundaries did not mean an end to resistance however, and the battalion actually encountered some of its fiercest firefights with insurgents attacking from bunkers and mosques. First Lieutenant Flanagan recalled,

> Moving on the 15th of November, crossed over Phase Line Jenna, and we started to meet our heaviest resistance and we started to get more eyes on the enemy at that point. Our Marines that were equipped with ACOGS [advanced combat optical gun sites] on their M16s and on their M4s, were actually, since we were moving so tactically fast, they were actually getting more confirmed kills than our snipers, because we were just—the snipers didn't have the time to set up and provide enough overwatch. Those guys with the ACOGS and the M203s were just locating enemy, moving from house-to-house and engaging those enemy. They had a lot of confirmed enemy kills that afternoon on 15 November, as we moved south.[291]

The 1st Battalion, 8th Marines, also relied on close air support to destroy the insurgent positions.

In northeast Fallujah, 1st Battalion, 3d Marines, continued clearing buildings in their quarter of the city. Sergeant Rafael Peralta, a platoon guide, had volunteered to assist his fellow Marines in the arduous task. After clearing several buildings, he and his squad entered a house where insurgents waiting in ambush opened fire. During the firefight, Sergeant Peralta was wounded in the crossfire between his Marines and insurgents. As the insurgents broke contact, they tossed a grenade in the room. Peralta's body absorbed the blast, saving the lives of several members of his squad. Peralta succumbed to his wounds and posthumously received the Navy Cross.[292]

On Fallujah's periphery, the 2d Brigade Combat Team (2d Brigade, 1st Cavalry Division), began to conduct a series of operations to disrupt insurgent activity. North of Fallujah, the Iraqi 6th Battalion, 3d Brigade, which had primarily operated traffic control points during the battle, conducted a cordon-and-search mission with 1st Battalion, 5th Cavalry Regiment, and detained 17 individuals. On the western side of the Euphrates River, a light armored vehicle from Task Force Wolfpack received a rocket-propelled grenade shot that penetrated the vehicle's armor while conducting patrols.[293]

16–17 November

In southeast Fallujah, Company I and Company K, 3d Battalion, 1st Marines, rejoined Company L, then prepared to attack south on the next day. Although activity was light, the battalion continued patrolling during the day and night and Company K lost another Marine from insurgent fire. In northwest Fallujah, 3d Battalion, 5th Marines, continued searching for insurgents and weapons while civil affairs teams continued supervising the removal of dead insurgents.[294]

Meanwhile, in the industrial district, Task Force 2-2 moved north again and began clearing the west side of the industrial district. "That last night fight, I think we destroyed any remnant of any organized resistance there had been," Newell recalled. "After that, the only guys we ran across were the ones that weren't smart enough to get out or couldn't. There was very little left after that point, but we still went building-to-building and room-to-room and went through every one of them. At that point, we started clearing the caches. A credit to the IIF [Iraqi Intervention Force] guys—who pulled up behind us—without us telling them to, they were re-clearing the buildings behind us."[295] During the clearing operations, Company A, 2d Battalion, 2d Infantry, discovered more weapons caches, including a vehicleborne IED factory and a control center with black flags indicating Abu Musab al-Zarqawi's headquarters.[296]

East of Task Force 2-2, 1st Battalion, 8th Marines, continued to locate weapons cache sites and record the locations of insurgent dead so that 1st Force Service Support Group or Red Crescent personnel could remove the bodies and give them a proper burial. During their searches, however, Marines continued to find groups of insurgents waiting in ambush. In one case, Company A encountered four insurgents in a house within 50 meters of Company A's base. As the Marines entered the house, they immediately engaged the insurgents, hit one, but then withdrew when an insurgent threw a fragmentation grenade at them.[297] After cordoning off the house, Company A's Marines fired two shoulder-launched, multipurpose assault weapons into the house. Unfazed by this attack, the insurgents refused to surrender. The company's linguist, First Lieutenant John V. Flanagan, then moved up to the corner of the house with an Arabic interpreter and informed the insurgents that the house was surrounded and ordered them to surrender. The insurgents responded with chants of Allahu Akbar ("God is great"), signifying they were not going to give up their position.[298] Thinking that the insurgents in the house may have been rigged with suicide explosive vests, the Marines backed off and killed the four insurgents by firing .50-caliber machine-gun rounds into the house.[299]

In northern Fallujah, Colonel Shupp's Marines reopened Fallujah's New Bridge. The event was attended by the overall Coalition commander General George W. Casey, USA. By this point the transition to stability operations had gained momentum. Lieutenant Colonel Malay's 3d Battalion, 5th Marines, established zones of responsibility for its companies throughout the northwestern districts of the city. Meanwhile, Colonel Tucker's Marines opened a humanitarian support center at the Fallujah government center and began providing humanitarian aid to civilians still in the city. At the same time, Colonel Ballard's civil affairs Marines moved into the gov-

ernment center and began to establish the 1st Marine Division's civil-military operations center. Civil affairs teams working with 3d Battalion, 5th Marines, opened the town of Saqlawiyah, where an estimated 50,000 Fallujan refugees were located, and delivered 18 tractor-trailer trucks full of food and supplies to the people. Civil affairs Marines also sent humanitarian aid to Fallujan refugees in Habbaniyah.[300]

A greater focus on stability operations did not mean that the task of fully securing the city had come to an end. In northeast Fallujah, 1st Battalion, 3d Marines, continued clearing its sector. Lieutenant Colonel Newell sent the headquarters section from Company A, 2d Battalion, 63d Armor, with two Bradley fighting vehicles, two tanks to assist the 1st Battalion, 3d Marines, and an attached Iraq Intervention Force platoon.[301] Company C, 1st Battalion, 3d Marines, came into frequent contact with bands of insurgents but suffered no casualties. On Fallujah's periphery, Major Miller's Company B, 1st Battalion, 23d Marines, attacked to clear the northwest sector of Task Force Wolfpack's area of operations in response to an ambush on Major Wittnam's Small Craft Company the day before. Miller's Marines faced minimal enemy contact and found one 120mm mortar prepositioned to fire at Task Force Wolfpack's position. Colonel James C. McConville's U.S. Army Apache helicopters flew through another day of heavy antiaircraft fire while patrolling Fallujah's boundaries. "We started to see that the anti-Iraqi forces (AIF) were really going after the aircraft," McConville recalled. "We had a sense that they really wanted to take an aircraft down.[302]

The following day in southwest Fallujah, Company K, 3d Battalion, 1st Marines, cleared continuously through the day and encountered the largest concentration of enemy forces in buildings near the intersection of Phase Line Isabel and Phase Line Isaac.[303] The battalion operations officer, Major Griffen, described the resistance as "dogged" and "determined" and noted that the "enemy were just not to be rooted out of their positions alive."[304] In one engagement, a squad from 2d Platoon, Company K, entered a house with the windows covered and came under heavy fire, injuring Lance Corporal Dane R. Shaffer. Marines extracted their injured comrade and then set up a cordon around the house and demolished it with a D9 bulldozer. When four insurgents fled to the roof of the house, nearby Marines from Company L killed three of them.[305] According to First Lieutenant John Jacobs, commander of 2d Platoon, Company K, the fourth insurgent "tried to jump off the roof and got hung up on a piece of rebar," where Marines shot him from below as "he was hanging there in midair."[306]

Marines from Company C, 1st Battalion, 3d Marines, look over a map during the advance into Fallujah.

Meanwhile, insurgents still inside the house shot at the D9 bulldozer as it began demolishing the house. "Then the roof came down," Jacobs recalled "and the shooting stopped."[307] During the engagements, Company K killed 29 insurgents who had fought in groups of 6 to 11, and sustained 2 friendly wounded in action. That night, 3d Battalion, 1st Marines, consolidated on Phase Line Isabel.[308]

In southeast Fallujah, Task Force 2-2 moved back up to the industrial area and started hunting for all the caches and the IED factories. To their west, Companies A and B, 1st Battalion, 8th Marines, finished attacking south and began clearing buildings in their areas along Fallujah's southern boundary.[309] Meanwhile, Company C continued to clear high-rise buildings northwest of Companies A and B, using engineers to conduct explosive breaches to get inside secured buildings. "Inside the buildings," Captain Bethea recalled, "we found Iraqis who were scared, who were holed up, and who were just seeking some means of assistance. And so, we directed 'em, gave them the instructions on where to go, and the times to go to get food and water, and then continued to clear in zone."[310]

"We realized that now the civilians have been in their houses for over a week," recalled Lieutenant Colonel Brandl. "They've complied with staying out of the fighting. We want to at least give them food and water, and we've set up, from 8 to 12 each day, being able to come to a food distribution point where I've got my Iraqi forces . . . [who] can pull out the foreign fighters pretty quickly."[311]

At Fallujah's government center, the civil-military operation center (known to Fallujans as the Fallujah Help Center) was operational and served as a coordination site among the U.S. and Iraqi military, the Iraqi people, Fallujah municipal workers, reconstruction contractors, and nongovernmental organizations. Civil Affairs Detachment 4-4 continued assessing the damage and requirements to remove rubble and begin reconstruction and restoration of essential services. After completing over 60 infrastructure assessments, the work to repair critical infrastructure, restore essential services, and clear rubble began in earnest. Meanwhile, Major General Natonski and his regimental commanders recognized that decisive operations in the city were nearing their completion. Colonel Shupp then met with his battalion

Battle for Fallujah

commanders to begin planning for Regimental Combat Team 1 to assume responsibility for the entire city as the rest of 1st Marine Division prepared to redeploy to their areas of responsibility throughout the rest of al-Anbar Province.[312]

18–19 November

In southwest Fallujah, 3d Battalion, 1st Marines, established company strong points that were staggered from the north to south across their sector. Company L remained in the extreme northwest. Company K was centered north to south along Phase Line Henry. Company I was in the southeastern most position. Lieutenant Colonel Buhl tasked each company to conduct detailed searches in what operations officer Major Griffin described as "to basically sterilize that city before the reoccupation by the residents so that we could eliminate any of the munitions that they might be able to make use of."[313] During these operations, Marines encountered few insurgents, but did engage some attempting to swim across the river from the peninsula.[314] They also captured some prisoners and numerous "massive" weapons caches that were too large to remove and had to be destroyed in place. Company K discovered one weapons cache that Major Griffin recalled was "right next to their firm base . . . an entire house stacked full of crates of 155mm artillery projectiles. Hand grenades, SA7s, rocket-propelled grenade[s] . . ."[315]

In southeast Fallujah, Task Force 2-2 continued to attack all the way south out of the city toward the canal looking for weapons caches, but Lieutenant Colonel Newell found "nothing out there but a minefield."[316] Meanwhile, after 10 days of continuous fighting, Lieutenant Colonel Brandl began to rotate his troops back to Camp Fallujah to rest, take showers, and eat hot food.[317] Captain Read M. Omohundro's Company B, 1st Battalion, 8th Marines, returned to the forward operating base while Captain Aaron M. Cunningham's Company A, 1st Battalion, 8th Marines, continued the house-to-house search finding small weapons caches and detaining some insurgents in the morning.[318] On the peninsula, one of Task Force Wolfpack's command and control light armored vehicles at the forward command post received a direct hit from a 107mm rocket as insurgents continued to attack soldiers and Marines. Fortunately, while the vehicle was immobilized, there were no casualties, and it was repaired the next day.[319]

The next day, 3d Battalion, 1st Marines, returned to the battalion command post at the train station north of the city.[320] First Lieutenant Jacobs noted, "that was the end of our gunfight."[321] Company K commander Captain Jent recalled, "I think there was definitely a feeling of accomplishment, and we were obviously physically tired, mentally—they were tired."[322]

In southeast Fallujah, Task Force 2-2 continued clearing beyond Fallujah's southern boundary. This would be the last full day of operations in the city for Task Force 2-2. To the west of Task Force 2-2, Company B, 1st Battalion, 8th Marines, began clearing their sector in southern Fallujah after having the day off. Soon thereafter, 1st Platoon Marines saw a group of military-age males walking with white flags, one of whom was smiling and waving to the Marines. A short time later, the platoon received fire from the same man. They went to the insurgents' position, where grenades killed two of 1st Platoon's Marines and their Iraqi interpreter, forcing the Marines to respond with artillery.[323] Meanwhile, Company C also continued conducting combat operations. Third Squad, 1st Platoon, Company C, departed friendly lines to patrol a designated section. At 0845, the squad discovered a weapons and medical cache in a mosque that contained medical supplies for 10,000 people, a rocket-propelled grenade launcher, a sniper scope, a PKM medium machine gun, and 7.62mm ammunition.[324]

At Fallujah's government center, the 4th Civil Affairs Group and the 1st Marine Division conducted a planning meeting to restore basic services and return citizens back to Fallujah. The three critical tasks assigned to Civil Affairs Detachment 4-4 were solving the city's standing water problem, restoring a supply of fresh water, and constructing three humanitarian assistance distribution sites in Fallujah.[325] Although Fallujah was becoming more secure, insurgent forces remained a threat in the areas around the city. "Not only did we take the fight to Fallujah," recalled Major General Natonski, "but we took it to the surrounding cities as well, with the intent of disrupting the enemy. Always on the offensive, always being aggressive. Not waiting for them to hit us, taking the fight to the enemy."[326] For example, Task Force Wolfpack attacked to clear the southeast zone where insurgents had continued attacking Coalition forces. The effort resulted in 1 enemy wounded-in-action and 52 detainees, and Company B, 1st Battalion, 23d Marines, also discovered a large ammo cache. The 2d Brigade Combat Team (2d Brigade, 1st Cavalry Division) also conducted a series of operations focusing on clearing insurgents in Saqlawiyah, Karmah, Nasser wa Salaam, Zaidon, and Ameriya. These operations tied in with the 24th Marine Expeditionary Unit's activities in North Babil Province.[327]

As most of the 1st Marine Division's assault force redeployed from Fallujah at the end of November, much work remained for those units remaining in the city. Here Marines from 3d Battalion, 5th Marines, guard Iraqis captured during a cordon-and-knock operation conducted in Fallujah in early December 2004.

Final Operations

On 20 November 2004, Task Force 2-7 and Task Force 2-2 withdrew from the city. Meanwhile, Regimental Combat Team 1 continued to rest, rearm, and redeploy in preparation for assuming sole occupation responsibilities for the entire city. At the government center, civil affairs began clearing rubbish and conducting infrastructure repairs. Civil Affairs Detachment 4-4 placed 27 6,000–10,000-gallon water tanks and 30 generators throughout the city as a temporary measure to provide fresh water and electricity while long-term repairs got underway. Iraqi water trucks refilled the tanks each day with fresh water.

At Camp Fallujah on 20 November, Lieutenant General Sattler hosted the first Fallujah reconstruction meeting between U.S. military leaders, Major General Abdul Qader Mohammed Jassim (the Iraqi military leader in Fallujah), and senior ministry representatives from the Iraqi interim government. While Major General Natonski focused on the battle, Lieutenant General Sattler worked with Multi-National Force-Iraq, Multi-National Corps-Iraq, and the other ministries of Iraq to support Fallujah's reconstruction.

On 24 November, I Marine Expeditionary Force, 1st Marine Division, and Iraqi planners completed a city resettlement plan to administer the flow of citizens into Fallujah. The plan called for five entry control points to restrict access into the city, four designed for citizens and one that was exclusively for government officials, contractors, and military.[328] The city was divided into 17 areas. That same day, the Iraqi Red Crescent Society established operations in an abandoned house in Fallujah, becoming the first nongovernmental organization to work in the city since the commencement of Operation Phantom Fury/al-Fajr. The Red Crescent gained entrance to Fallujah under the pretense of delivering humanitarian assistance supplies to the Hadrah Mosque, but instead had a different agenda. Soon after arriving, they used ambulances with loudspeakers to call people into the street. About 100 military-age males answered the call and found their way to the abandoned house under the protection of Red Crescent in violation of a city-wide curfew and order that all military-age males would be detained and questioned. To make matters worse, the Marines then observed several ambulances leaving the city with military-age males. With the aim of stopping enemy fighters

Battle for Fallujah

Photo by LCpl Daniel J. Klein

Marines from Company C, 1st Battalion, 3d Marines, stop at a building corner to inspect the surrounding area while on patrol in Fallujah. An AAV-7A1 amphibious assault vehicle can be partially seen on the left.

from escaping, Lieutenant Colonel Leonard J. DeFrancisci confronted the Red Crescent, stating that they could not be an insurgent rescue service. The Marines knew from previous operations that the organization used ambulances to transport enemy fighters and supplies.[329]

By 28 November, soldiers and Marines had discovered 346 major weapons caches, about one in every three city blocks, eight hostage sites (three of which were execution/torture chambers), 653 IEDs, and 26 IED and vehicleborne IED factories. They also noted that 63 of 133 recognized mosques had been used as fighting positions or weapons caches and documented 24 separate cases of foreign fighter involvement. That same day Marines held the second reconstruction meeting between U.S. military leaders and Iraqi leaders at Camp Fallujah. During the meeting, Iraqi leaders insisted that 15 December be the date to reopen Fallujah to civilians. Two days later, Iraqi Interim Prime Minister Ayad Allawai visited the city. Allawi had wanted to open the city to resettlement on 1 December, but Lieutenant General Sattler convinced Generals Casey and Metz to delay until the city was safer and its infrastructure better restored.[330]

On 6 December, Captain Henegar, civil affairs team leader supporting 3d Battalion, 5th Marines, began an early intervention project to hire local Iraqis to clean up the city. This project commenced with two teams of 10 Iraqis, each consisting of one foreman leading nine workers equipped with brooms, shovels, and wheelbarrows. They started by cleaning the entry control points and worked their way into the city cleaning the massive amounts of rubble that resulted from the battle. The foremen received $10 (U.S.) an hour and the workers $6 (U.S.) an hour. Civil affairs initiated numerous projects such as this to provide jobs and focus attention of the Iraqis on rebuilding their city. Marines called them "muj" working parties because they consisted of many former enemy fighters who laid down their arms and took up brooms. Civil affairs hired as many local contractors as possible, but the extensive reconstruction projects requiring heavy equipment came from Baghdad.[331]

On 9 December, Regimental Combat Team 1 assumed full control of Fallujah. On 11 December, Marines constructed five entry control points around the city to manage the flow of civilians back into the city. Civil affairs teams supporting each battalion established three hu-

Photo by SSgt Jonathan C. Knauth

Hospital Corpsman 3d Class David Naderman of 1st Battalion, 8th Marines, points his M9 pistol toward a courtyard suspected of housing insurgents in Fallujah during the latter half of Operation al-Fajr.

manitarian assistance distribution sites at key junctures in the city to provide food rations, blankets, water, humanitarian aid payments, and other necessities to returning residents. In the Jolan District, 3d Battalion, 5th Marines, constructed a humanitarian aid site at the Jolan Park.[332] Sattler noted that "these sites eventually supplied humanitarian relief to 87,620 residents." Additionally, Civil Affairs Detachment 4-4 completed the assessments of the city's infrastructure and services, which included medical facilities, water treatment plants, power plants, sewer pumping stations, roads, bridges, schools, government buildings and services, police stations, fire departments, businesses, banks, gas stations, and housing.[333]

Meanwhile, Marines continued to encounter insurgents in all sectors of the city. The residual insurgent presence slowed reconstruction progress since the fights to detain them kept most contractors out of the city.[334] On the morning of 12 December, just before 1200, for example, Task Force Bruno came into contact with 15–20 insurgents in a building in north Fallujah. In the course of the fight, several Marines became trapped inside the building by the intense enemy fire. Third Battalion, 5th Marines' executive officer, Major Desgrosseilliers, rushed into the building just as an enemy grenade landed at his feet. He shielded his trapped Marines from the grenade with his own body. The blast did not kill him, but did leave him with significant shrapnel wounds. Despite this, Desgrosseilliers led his Marines out of the building through another door and then led them in an assault on the house that killed several insurgents. The task force was joined by 1st Platoon, Company K, and a section of

tanks as it pressed the attack against insurgents attempting to flee across rooftops and balconies. When it was finally over, Task Force Bruno had killed 20 insurgents and suffered 7 wounded-in-action.[335]

Meanwhile, the remainder of Company K, 3d Battalion, 5th Marines, continued its final clearing operations in northern Fallujah. By 1500, company commander Captain McNulty concluded that the effort to fully clear the area would take longer than expected and decided to postpone the final portion of the operation until the following morning. McNulty sent his tanks to rearm and refit and ordered his company to move from their present location to a new headquarters, a school previously utilized for the same purpose by 1st Battalion, 3d Marines' Company A.

To prepare for the cold night, 3d Platoon and 2d Platoon advanced on an unsecured block of nearby buildings to recover bedding. There was some disagreement over this order, as it meant clearing buildings without the usual coordination and support. Furthermore, sleeping bags and ponchos were available from nearby amphibious assault vehicles.[336] Nevertheless, the two platoons followed through with their original plan. As they cleared the buildings in the northeast side of the block, Corporal Ian W. Stewart moved up the stairs of a building with his 9mm pistol toward the second floor while his fellow Marines cleared the bottom floor. Insurgents struck soon after he reached the top of the stairs, killing Stewart and throwing grenades down the staircase. Lance Corporal Chad Pioske and Corporal David P. Cisineros attempted to get to Corporal Stewart's body, but enemy fire prevented them from doing so.[337]

When news of Stewart's death reached Sergeant Jeffrey L. Kirk and the platoon sergeant Staff Sergeant Melvin L. Blazer Jr., they worked to isolate Stewart's building and attempted to find another point of entry. As Sergeant Kirk maneuvered alone north in a very narrow alley, he was shot and killed by insurgents believed to be firing out the second floor window of the building. In an adjoining building, two Marines were wounded and subsequently evacuated. Meanwhile, Staff Sergeant Blazer led Marines into another building and was killed by insurgents at the top of the stairs while moving toward the rooftop. Covering their actions with squad automatic weapon fire, the Marines recovered Staff Sergeant Blazer's body and evacuated the building.[338]

Reaching the patio of a building adjoining the one in which Corporal Stewart had been killed, Lance Corporal Pioske engaged and killed five insurgents while five Marines around him sustained injuries. As the Marines evacuated their wounded to a nearby casualty collection

Battle for Fallujah

Marines of 1st Battalion, 8th Marines, search a building suspected of housing insurgents during Operation al-Fajr.

point, elements of the combined antiarmor team arrived on the scene and began to assist with isolating the block. The platoon commanders also arrived with the remaining squad leaders and amphibious assault vehicles and began to cordon the downstairs of the building where Corporal Stewart's body still lay. Captain McNulty arrived, received a situation report, and then began coordination to bomb the remainder of the buildings in the block.[339]

Before the airstrike could commence, however, Company K needed to recover Corporal Stewart's body. Once the Marines of Company K cleared the adjacent buildings, Corporal Jason S. Clairday led a squad into the building where the body remained on the second floor. As soon as he moved through the door, he was shot and wounded in both arms and both legs. Refusing medical assistance, Clairday moved to the front of the line of advance and attacked one room as other Marines moved to the room containing Corporal Stewart's body where they killed three insurgents. In the course of attacking another room, Clairday was mortally wounded along with Lance Corporal Hilario F. Lopez. The remainder of the squad

killed the rest of the insurgents and evacuated the casualties to amphibious assault vehicles.[340] Corporal Clairday would posthumously receive the Navy Cross for his actions during this engagement.

With the buildings evacuated, Captain McNulty isolated the block with tanks as amphibious tracked vehicles and the Combined Antiarmor Team covered Company K's withdrawal. He then called in an airstrike that flattened the buildings with joint direct attack munitions (JDAMs) from U.S. Air Force General Dynamics F-16 Fighting Falcons. Fighting continued around the block through the night, and ultimately a second airstrike was called in to demolish the block. Company K estimated that it killed 30 insurgents in the struggle for it.[341]

On the morning of 14 December, Lieutenant Colonel Malay's 3d Battalion, 5th Marines, continued clearing operations in northeast Fallujah. As the companies moved south to north, Sergeant Eric J. Copsetta's squad climbed up to the rooftop of a house to clear it. After throwing a stun grenade down the ladder well and detecting no movement, a Marine and an Iraq Intervention Force sol-

November - December 2004

dier went downstairs and cleared the kitchen while another Marine with an Iraqi soldier followed. An insurgent shot Corporal Michael D. Anderson Jr. from the side as he kicked in the door to a room. The Iraqi soldier fell back as Hospital Corpsman Second Class Nicholas Cook and Lance Corporal Bradley A. Balak moved into position on the ladder well and fired suppression fire into the doorway to the room. Meanwhile, Corporal Van Doorn's squad finished clearing and began isolating the house. Sergeant Elber Navarro arrived with an amphibious tracked vehicle that broke through the front gate, which allowed his squad to enter the house. Seeing Corporal Anderson in the doorway of the room with the enemy, Sergeant Navarro's squad cleared every room except for the room with the enemy. With several Marines in the house, the insurgents in the room had no escape. Sergeant Navarro approached the room and threw multiple fragmentation and high-concentrate smoke grenades, and then threw an incendiary grenade that set the room on fire. Captain McNulty arrived and pulled Corporal Anderson's body to the bathroom away from the enemy as Sergeant Navarro entered the room and killed two or three insurgents at close range, and then withdrew as the enemy fired automatic weapons and threw grenades into the hallway and the kitchen, which caused several Marines to withdraw from the kitchen into the yard where Lance Corporal Rouse took a large piece of shrapnel to the leg.[342]

With the room fully on fire, Sergeant Navarro covered Captain McNulty's move back to Sergeant Navarro's position. After further assessment of the situation, Sergeant Navarro threw another incendiary grenade into the room to ensure its destruction. An insurgent attempted to flee the room and was shot repeatedly at close range by Sergeant Navarro and Captain McNulty. With this complete, Captain McNulty determined the threat to be eliminated and proceeded back to the bathroom with Sergeant Navarro to Corporal Anderson's body. During this time, the battalion commander, Lieutenant Colonel Malay, and his security detachment arrived and entered the house believing that Captain McNulty might be wounded or killed because he was not responding to questions from outside the house. Captain McNulty was partially deaf from the multiple grenade explosions. Lieutenant Colonel Malay and Sergeant Navarro shot a surviving insurgent who attempted to flee out the front door. As Marines exchanged fire with surviving insurgents inside the burning room, one ran out of the room and up the stairs where Lance Corporal Balak killed him. Sergeant Navarro threw one last fragmentation grenade into the room before Marines recovered Corporal Anderson's body.[343]

Elsewhere on 14 December 2004, I MEF released Operations Order 001-04, which assigned the 4th Civil Affairs Group as the main effort and detailed the functional responsibilities for all of the I MEF subordinate commanders. To ensure a smooth transition to Phase IV operations, Lieutenant General Sattler appointed Brigadier General Dennis J. Hejlik, deputy commanding general, I MEF, as the executive agent to oversee the security, stability, reconstruction, and resettlement efforts in Fallujah. Colonel Ballard, 4th Civil Affairs Group commander, was responsible for ensuring the government met the basic needs of the people, and Rear Admiral Raymond K. Alexander, I MEF Engineering Group commander, was responsible for coordinating all projects in the city with the Iraqi government. The following day, however, on 15 December, Marines decided to postpone the return of civilians into the city because they recognized that there were still insurgents moving freely and there was too much unexploded ordnance. On 21 December 2004, the Iraqi interim government announced that Fallujans could reenter the city on 23 December 2004 for the resettlement of Fallujah.[344]

Reentry of Civilians and Continued Restoration Operations

On 23 December 2004, Marines opened the city to civilian resettlement. At each of the five primary entry control points, Marines with military working dog teams worked alongside Iraqi soldiers from the Iraqi Public Order Battalion searching vehicles and people before allowing them to enter the city.[345] As residents entered the city, Marines and Iraqi soldiers carefully scrutinized military-age males while female soldiers and Marines searched Iraqi women. Once physically searched, Marines further screened and registered all males, collecting their names, birth dates, places of birth, religious affiliations, height, weight, and hair and eye colors, along with biometric data that included a scanned fingerprint of the left index finger, an iris scan of the right eye, and a digital photograph. The biometric automated tool set conducted a background inspection that included comparing facial features, iris scans, and index finger scans against known or suspected insurgents. If the system found a match it would show up red, and at that point, a human exploitation team would take the individual for questioning. If the computer check came back clear, the individual received an identification card so that on future trips in and out of the city he would not have to go through the complete biometric screening process again. Despite the slow process, Marines were not willing to sacrifice security to speed up reentry.[346] By the

Marines from Company I, 3d Battalion, 5th Marines, rest in a building in Fallujah during the assault on the city. They are equipped with 5.56mm M249 Squad Automatic Weapons. The firearm between the two Marines on the left is a 5.56mm M4 carbine.

end of the day, 1600 hours, 165 vehicles and nearly 1,000 citizens entered the city, along with 100 contractors and workers, and according to a Central Command press release, "Only 1 person was detained and 16 were turned away due to not providing proof of residency."[347]

In northeast Fallujah, as the first refugees returned on 23 December, Task Force Bruno came under heavy enemy fire from 30 insurgents while the task force continued to clear the last sections of northern Fallujah. During the more than eight-hour engagement, Marines cleared several enemy strong points and endured intense fighting. Major Desgrosseilliers was wounded by shrapnel but led his Marines in the attack and directed tank main gunfire on the building until the insurgents were killed. He personally killed insurgents as he cleared several rooms, and exposed himself to direct enemy fire and helped drag a seriously wounded Marine to safety. With this last major action, 3d Battalion, 5th Marines, had defeated the last group of insurgents in the city. However, Task Force Bruno suffered 3 killed-in-action and 18 wounded-in-action. Sergeant James A. Kraft and Corporal Jeremiah W. Workman

would receive the Navy Cross for their actions, and two others would receive Silver Stars.[348] According to Colonel Shupp, Marines determined that these insurgents had previously received humanitarian assistance from Regimental Combat Team 7.[349]

By 31 December, civilians had returned to the Jolan and al-Andalus Districts, north of Highway 10. However, in the old foreign fighter strongholds of southern Fallujah, 3d Battalion, 1st Marines, saw few civilians return to the city because they had long been displaced by foreign fighters. On 5 January, 2,500 residents passed through entry control point five, and nearly 50,000 residents had reentered Fallujah since Marines opened the city to resettlement. It was unclear how many actually stayed because many found their homes unlivable. However, residents received humanitarian assistance as civil affairs continued working on reconstruction and restoring essential services such as running water and electricity. By the middle of January 2005, Fallujah was noticeably different. All neighborhoods were open to resettlement, and the markets in the al-Andalus District were doing

A HMMWV from Task Force 2-7 patrols a highway on the outskirts of Fallujah in November 2004.

business again. I Marine Expeditionary Force continued to work diligently to ensure that residents of Fallujah and al-Anbar Province could vote on 30 January. With Fallujah free from insurgents' control, residents felt a renewed sense of security and felt comfortable enough to begin reporting criminal and insurgent activity to authorities.[350]

Conclusions

The U.S.-led Coalition waged two battles to clear and secure the city of Fallujah from insurgent control. The first ended quickly and failed to extricate the insurgency from the city. For a number of reasons, including political pressures from above, a hostile popular reaction, and lack of time to adequately prepare, the 1st Marine Division was unable to secure the city and root out all insurgent activity. Indeed, Fallujah, which had been particularly hostile and volatile before the first battle, became an even more problematic source of insurgent activity following the failed offensive. The failure to signal resolve gave the insurgency an unprecedented victory over the Coalition and the still nascent Iraqi government.[351]

The Second Battle of Fallujah was one of the largest engagements of the Iraq War and marked a significant victory for the Coalition. The United States suffered 82 killed-in-action and over 600 wounded-in-action. Seventy-six of those killed were Marines. Iraqi forces suffered 6 dead and 55 wounded. Estimated insurgent casualties were 2,000 killed and 1,200 captured.[352] The second attempt to take the city succeeded largely because planners paid close attention to the mistakes made during the first battle. I MEF took the time to shape conditions on the battlefield to optimize U.S. advantages and lay the groundwork for an effective assault. The expeditionary force conducted a range of psychological and information operations to undermine insurgent morale and encourage civilians to vacate the city. I MEF also ensured that it had enough forces to not only attack and clear the city, but also to encircle and seal it, preventing large numbers of insurgents from escaping. Operation Phantom Fury/al-Fajr called for a significant combined arms force of four infantry battalions (reinforced with armored sections), four mechanized battalions, a light armored reconnaissance battalion, and supporting aviation and

Battle for Fallujah

logistics units. Securing the approaches to the battlefield also required the deployment of a British armored battalion and a Marine expeditionary unit.

From 7 November to 20 December, the Marines and soldiers of the expeditionary force cleared the city, block-by-block, house-by-house, room-by-room. The battle was an example of successful joint operations. Soldiers and Marines fought alongside each other, working closely as they advanced through the narrow city streets. They were supported by Army and Marine helicopters, as well as Marine, Air Force, and Navy fixed-wing aircraft.

In many ways the Second Battle of Fallujah was atypical of the majority of engagements fought during the Marine campaign in al-Anbar. Contrary to the popular image of combat in the Middle East, the Marines and soldiers at Fallujah frequently fought in the rain. For the most part, the battles that defined this campaign were small-unit actions involving battalion and company-size formations. Another difference between Fallujah and subsequent battles was the role of Iraqi forces. Beginning in late 2006, many of the battles for al-Anbar involved Marines fighting alongside local tribal militias against al-Qaeda in Iraq. Those alliances, which emerged out of the 2006–7 al-Anbar Awakening, were still two years away when the Marines and soldiers of I MEF waged their grueling fight to take Fallujah. While Iraqi military forces fought alongside both Marines and soldiers in Fallujah, they did so largely in supporting roles.

While there were differences, the struggle for Fallujah also shared many characteristics of the other battles that defined the al-Anbar campaign. First, the enemy force the United States faced in Fallujah was similar to the other insurgent groups operating throughout the province: an eclectic mix of Iraqi nationalists, Islamists, and international fighters drawn together by the common objective of expelling the United States from Iraq and destabilizing the new Iraqi government. The insurgents displayed considerable organizational skills, were well-equipped, and were able to devise a range of tactics against Coalition forces that compensated for their disadvantages in the face of the Coalition's superiority in terms of technology and firepower. The Marines and soldiers advancing into Fallujah faced insurgents armed with assault rifles, machine guns, and rocket-propelled grenades. Throughout the battle, insurgents also utilized improvised explosive devices which proved effective against personnel and equipment alike. They relied on ambush tactics, lying in wait in buildings, faking surrender, or faking death. They readily used civilians as shields, blended into the population, and were willing to die rather than surrender. All of these characteristics were common to the insurgents Marines and soldiers would face throughout al-Anbar and Iraq as a whole.

By January 2005, the city was secure enough for Iraqis to go to the polls to vote on the composition of a new constituent assembly. The struggle to secure al-Anbar was not over however. Tough fights awaited the Multi-National Force-West at al-Qaim, ar-Ramadi, and other cities stretching along the Euphrates from the Syrian border to Baghdad. However, Fallujah, once the central hub of the insurgency, had been largely neutralized as a source of resistance to the Iraqi government and U.S. forces operating in Iraq. That it remained so for the remainder of the al-Anbar campaign stands as a testament to the soldiers, sailors, airmen, and Marines who successfully worked together during those hard-fought months at the end of 2004.

Appendix A
Operation al-Fajr: Principal Units

Unit	Commanding Officer
I Marine Expeditionary Force	LtGen John F. Sattler
24th Marine Expeditionary Unit	Col Robert J. Johnson
31st Marine Expeditionary Unit	Col Walter L. Miller Jr.

GROUND COMBAT ELEMENT

1st Marine Division	MajGen Richard F. Natonski
Regimental Combat Team 1	Col Michael A. Shupp
3d Battalion, 1st Marines	LtCol Willard A. Buhl
3d Battalion, 5th Marines	LtCol Patrick J. Malay
Task Force 2-7 (2d Battalion, 7th Cavalry) (U.S. Army)	LtCol James Rainey, USA
Regimental Combat Team 7	Col Craig A. Tucker
1st Battalion, 8th Marines	LtCol Gareth F. Brandl
1st Battalion, 3d Marines	LtCol Michael R. Ramos
Task Force 2-2 (2d Battalion, 2d Infantry) (U.S. Army)	LtCol Peter Newell, USA
2d Brigade Combat Team, (2d Brigade, 1st Cavalry Division) (U.S. Army)	Col Michael Formica, USA
Task Force 1-5 Cavalry (1st Battalion, 5th Cavalry) (U.S. Army)	LtCol Myles M. Miyamasu, USA
Task Force 1-5 Infantry (1st Battalion, 5th Infantry) (U.S. Army)	LtCol Todd McCaffrey, USA
3d Light Armored Reconnaissance Battalion (Task Force Wolfpack)	LtCol Steve Dinauer

AVIATION COMBAT ELEMENT

3d Marine Aircraft Wing	MajGen Keith J. Stalder
Marine Aircraft Group 16	Col Guy M. Close
Marine All-Weather Fighter Attack Squadron 242	LtCol Kevin M. Iiams
Marine Attack Squadron 311	LtCol C. A. Arnold
Marine Light Attack Helicopter Squadron 169	LtCol Lloyd A. Wright
Marine Light Attack Helicopter Squadron 367	LtCol Stephen W. Hall
Marine Medium Helicopter Squadron 268	LtCol Davis S. Foy
Marine Heavy Helicopter Squadron 361	LtCol Anthony L. Winters
Marine Wing Support Squadron 37	Col Juan G. Ayala
Marine Air Control Group 38	Col Ron R. McFarland
Marine Unmanned Aerial Vehicle Squadron 1	LtCol John H. Newman

COMBAT SUPPORT ELEMENT

1st Force Service Support Group	BGen Richard S. Kramlich
Combat Service Support Group 11	Col David B. Reist
Combat Service Support Group 15	Col Michael E. Kampsen
I Marine Expeditionary Force Engineer Group	RAdm Raymond K. Alexander

Appendix B

Operation al-Fajr: The Fallujah Assault Regiments

Regimental Combat Team 1 (1st Marines)
Commanding Officer: Col Michael Shupp

Company C, 2d Tank Battalion	Capt Robert J. Bodisch Jr.
Company B, 2d Assault Amphibian Battalion	Capt William E. O'Brien
Battery M, 4th Battalion, 14th Marines	Capt Milton K. Parsons
Small Craft Company	Maj Daniel J. Wittnam

3d Battalion, 5th Marines

Commanding Officer	LtCol Patrick J. Malay
Executive Officer	Maj Todd S. Degrosseilliers
Company I	Capt Brian R. Chontosh
Company K	Capt Andrew J. McNulty
Company L	Capt Eduardo C. Batanga
Weapons Company	Capt Thomas Knowl

3d Battalion, 1st Marines

Commanding Officer	LtCol Willard A. Buhl
Executive Officer	Maj Clark E. Watson
Company I	Capt Brett A. Clark
Company K	Capt Timothy J. Jent
Company L	Capt Brian G. Heatherman
Weapons Company	Capt Robert Belknap II

Task Force 2-7 (2d Battalion, 7th Cavalry, U.S. Army)

Commanding Officer	LtCol James E. Rainey, USA
Executive Officer	Maj Scott Jackson, USA
Company A, 2d Battalion, 7th Cavalry	Capt Edward S. Twaddell III, USA
Company C, 2d Battalion, 7th Cavalry	Capt Christopher P. Brooke, USA
Company C, 3d Battalion, 8th Cavalry	Capt Peter C. Glass, USA
Company B, 215th Forward Support Battalion	Capt Jake Brown, USA

Regimental Combat Team 7 (7th Marines)
Commanding Officer: Col Craig A. Tucker

Company A, 3d Light Armored Reconnaissance Battalion	Capt Michael R. Nakonieczny
Company A, 2d Tank Battalion	Capt Christopher V. Meyers
Company C, 3d Assault Amphibian Battalion	Capt Scott M. Conway
Battery C, 1st Battalion, 12th Marines	Capt John F. Kesterson

1st Battalion, 8th Marines

Commanding Officer	LtCol Gareth F. Brandl
Executive Officer	Maj Mark E. Winn
Company A	Capt Aaron Cunningham
Company B	Capt Read M. Omohundro
Company C	Capt Theodore Bethea
Weapons Company	Capt Stephen Kahn

1st Battalion, 3d Marines

Commanding Officer	LtCol Michael R. Ramos
Executive Officer	Major Andrew A. Kostic
Company A	Capt Lee A. Johnson
Company B	Capt Jer J. Garcia
Company C	Capt Thomas Tennant
Weapons Company	Capt Derek Wastilla

Task Force 2-2 (2d Battalion, 2d Infantry, U.S. Army)

Commanding Officer	LtCol Peter A. Newell, USA
Executive Officer	Captain Erik Krivda, USA
Company A, 2d Battalion, 2d Infantry	Capt Sean P. Sims Maj Doug Walter, USA
Company A, 2d Battalion, 63d Armor	Capt Neil S. Prakash, USA
F Troop, 4th Cavalry	Capt Kirk Mayfield, USA

Battle for Fallujah

Appendix C

Recipients of the Navy Cross for Actions during Operation al-Fajr

Name	Date of Action
LCpl Christopher S. Adlesperger	10 November 2004
Sgt Aubrey L. McDade Jr.	11 November 2004
1stSgt Bradley A. Kasal	13 November 2004
Cpl Robert J. Mitchell Jr.	13 November 2004
Sgt Rafael Peralta	15 November 2004
Cpl Dominic D. Esquibel	25 November 2004
Cpl Jason S. Clairday	12 December 2004
Cpl Jeremiah W. Workman	23 December 2004
Sgt James A. Kraft	23 December 2004

Appendix D

Operation al-Fajr: Chronology of Events

31 March 2004	Insurgents ambush and kill four Blackwater contractors while they are travelling through Fallujah.
4 April 2004	I Marine Expeditionary Force (I MEF) commences Operation Vigilant Resolve in an attempt to secure the city and apprehend those responsible for the 31 March murders.
9 April 2004	U.S. Central Command orders the suspension of offensive operations in Fallujah.
30 April 2004	Operation Vigilant Resolve officially ends. Fallujah is largely under insurgent control.
29 August 2004	MajGen Richard F. Natonski assumes command of the 1st Marine Division.
September–October 2004	I MEF initiates and conducts preliminary operations, known as Phase I, or "shaping," operations against insurgents in Fallujah.
12 September 2004	LtGen John F. Sattler assumes command of I MEF.
26 October 2004	I MEF issues order for Operation Phantom Fury.
1 November 2004	I MEF holds confirmation brief for the pending assault on Fallujah.
5 November 2004	2d Brigade Combat Team (2d Brigade, 1st Cavalry Division) takes up positions outside Fallujah to help seal the city.
7 November 2004	I MEF initiates and conducts Phase II, or "enhanced shaping," operations against insurgents in Fallujah.
8 November 2004	I MEF begins offensive operations against insurgents in the city of Fallujah.
9 November 2004	Task Force 2-7 secures Jolan Park.
10 November 2004	Task Force 2-7 seizes the two principal crossings over the Euphrates (Blackwater Bridge and New Bridge).
	Regimental Combat Team 1 and Regimental Combat Team 7 seize and secure Highway 10 (Main Supply Route Michigan).
11 November 2004	1st Battalion, 3d Marines, and Task Force 2-7 continue advance into southwestern Fallujah.
	1st Battalion, 8th Marines, and Task Force 2-2 continue advance into Fallujah's industrial district.
13 November 2004	Having achieved the initial objectives of Operation al-Fajr, 1st Marine Division begins the methodical clearing of the city.
	Marines from 3d Battalion, 1st Marines, become engaged in a bloody firefight for what becomes known as the "House from Hell."
16 November 2004	Fallujah's New Bridge is officially reopened.
20–25 November 2004	Elements of the Fallujah assault force, including the two Army battalions and Task Force Wolfpack, redeploy to other positions in al-Anbar Province as Regimental Combat Team 1 takes over clearing operations in the city.
9–16 December 2004	3d Battalion, 5th Marines, engages insurgents in a number of heavy firefights throughout northwest Fallujah.
24 December 2004	Regimental Combat Team 1 begins reintroducing civilians to Fallujah.

Notes

1. For histories of the Iraq War before the arrival of I Marine Expeditionary Force (I MEF) in al-Anbar, see Gregory Fontenot and E. J. Degen, *On Point: The United States Army in Operation Iraqi Freedom* (Fort Leavenworth, KS: Combat Studies Institute Press, 2004); Col Nicholas E. Reynolds, *U.S. Marines in Iraq, 2003: Basrah, Baghdad and Beyond* (Quantico, VA: History Division, United States Marine Corps, 2007); Donald P. Wright and Col Timothy R. Reese, *On Point II: Transition to the New Campaign: The United States Army in Operation IRAQI FREEDOM, May 2003–January 2005* (Fort Leavenworth, KS: Combat Studies Institute Press, 2008); Michael R. Gordon and Gen Bernard E. Trainor, *Cobra II: The Inside Story of the Invasion and Occupation of Iraq* (New York: Pantheon Books, 2006). For antisecular activity in Fallujah during the Baath era, see Ahmed S. Hashim, *Insurgency and Counter-Insurgency in Iraq* (Ithaca: Cornell University Press, 2006), 25.

2. LtGen James T. Conway intvw, 21 June 2005 and 7 July 2005, in *Al-Anbar Awakening: Volume I, American Perspectives, U.S. Marines and Counterinsurgency in Iraq, 2004-2009*, ed. CWO-4 Timothy S. McWilliams and LtCol Kurtis P. Wheeler (Quantico: Marine Corps University Press, 2009), 42–43; Gen James N. Mattis intvw, 17 June 2009, in *Al-Anbar Awakening: Volume I*, 22–28; Thomas E. Ricks, *Fiasco: The American Military Adventure in Iraq* (New York: Penguin Books, 2006), 313–20.

3. Kenneth W. Estes, *U.S. Marines in Iraq, 2004-2005: Into the Fray* (Washington, DC: History Division, United States Marine Corps, 2011), 31; Bing West, *No True Glory: A Frontline Account of the Battle of Fallujah* (New York: Bantam, 2005), 58–60.

4. Estes, *Into the Fray*, 31–32; West, *No True Glory*, 58–64; Mattis intvw; Conway intvw.

5. Estes, *Into the Fray*, 31–52; Maj Alfred B. Connable, "The Massacre That Wasn't," in *U.S. Marines in Iraq, 2004-2008: Anthology and Annotated Bibliography*, ed. Nicholas J. Schlosser (Washington, DC: History Division, United States Marine Corps, 2010), 75–81.

6. Estes, *Into the Fray*, 40; West, *No True Glory*, 210–20, 233–50.

7. See maps and descriptions in Estes, *Into the Fray*, 29–30; West, *No True Glory*, 13–14; Dick Camp, *Operation Phantom Fury: The Assault and Capture of Fallujah, Iraq* (Minneapolis: Zenith Press, 2009), 11–13.

8. Hashim, *Insurgency and Counter-Insurgency in Iraq*, 23–29; Edwin O. Rueda, "Tribalism in the Al Anbar Province," *Marine Corps Gazette* 90, no. 10 (2006); Faleh Abdul-Jabar, "Sheikhs and Ideologues: Deconstruction and Reconstruction of Tribes under Patrimonial Totalitarianism in Iraq, 1968–1998," in *Tribes and Power: Nationalism and Ethnicity in the Middle East*, ed. Faleh Abdul-Jabar and Hosham Dawod (London: Saqi, 2003), 69–109.

9. Hashim, *Insurgency and Counterinsurgency*, 142–44; *In Their Own Words: Voices of Jihad*, compiled and commentary by David Aaron (Santa Monica, CA: RAND Corporation, 2008), 243; Mary Anne Weaver, "The Short, Violent Life of Abu Musab al-Zarqawi," *The Atlantic*, July/August 2006; Benjamin Bahney, Howard T. Shatz, Carroll Ganier, Renny McPherseon, Barbara Sude, with Sarah Beth Elson, and Ghassan Schbley, *An Economic Analysis of the Financial Records of al-Qa'ida in Iraq* (Santa Monica, CA: RAND Corporation, 2010), 13.

10. Hashim, *Insurgency and Counterinsurgency*, 44.

11. Conway intvw; Mattis intvw; MajGen Richard F. Natonski intvw, 16 March 2005, in *Al-Anbar Awakening: Volume I*, 89–96; Hashim, *Insurgency and Counterinsurgency*, 43; LtGen John F. Sattler and LtCol Daniel H. Wilson, "Operation Al Fajr: The Battle of Fallujah: Part II," in *U.S. Marines in Iraq 2004–2008: Anthology and Annotated Bibliography*," 95–103; Jeffery Gettlemen, "The Re-Báathification of Falluja," *The New York Times Sunday Magazine*, 24 June 2004, 55; Karl Vick, "Fallujah Group Comes to Table," *The Washington Post*, 7 October 2004, A-14.

12. Operational Environment–Iraq: Critical Events Assessment OIF, 20 September 2004, info.publicintelligence.net/Fallujah.pdf; Col Michael M. Walker intvw, 24 March 2009 (Marine Corps Historical Center, Quantico, VA, hereafter MCHC, Quantico, VA); Hashim, *Insurgency and Counter-insurgency*, 36, 44–45; Sattler and Wilson, "Operation Al Fajr"; Malkasian, "Signaling Resolve, Democratization, and the First Battle of Fallujah," *Journal of Strategic Studies* 29 (2006): 423–52; Beth Gardiner, "Iraq Won't Allow Fallujah to Remain in Insurgent Control," Associated Press, 30 September 2004.

13. John F. Sattler HQMC Biography, https://slsp.manpower .usmc.mil/GOSA/Biographies/rptBiography.asp?PERSON_I D=40&PERSON_TYPE=General.

14. Col Rod Andrew Jr., *U.S. Marines in Battle: An-Nasiriyah 23 March–2 April 2003* (Washington, DC: History Division, United States Marine Corps, 2009).

15. LtCol Willard Buhl intvw, 28 October 2004 (MCHC, Quantico, VA); LtGen Richard F. Natonski comments on draft MS (MCHC, Quantico, VA).

16. LtGen Thomas F. Metz, LtCol Mark W. Garrett, Lt Col James E. Hutton, and LtCol Timothy W. Bush, U.S. Army, "Massing Effects in the Information Domain: A Case Study of Aggressive Information Operations," *Military Review*, May–June 2006; McWilliams and Wheeler, *Al-Anbar Awakening, Volume I*, 80–81.

17. Patrecia Slayden Hollis, "Second Battle of Fallujah—Urban Operations in a New Kind of War," *Field Artillery*, March-April 2006; Sattler and Wilson, "Operation Al Fajr."

18. Col Jenny Holbert intvw, 24 February 2010 (MCHC, Quantico, VA); Natonski comments.

19. LtCol John R. Way intvw with LtGen John F. Sattler, 8 April 2005 (MCHC, Quantico, VA); BGen Joseph F. Dunford intvw, 18 December 2006 (MCHC, Quantico, VA); Sattler and Wilson, "Operation Al-Fajr"; Natonski comments.

20. Col Leonard J. DeFrancisci comments on draft MS (MCHC, Quantico, VA); Regimental Combat Team 1, hereafter RCT-1, Command Chronology, hereafter ComdC, October 2004. Unless otherwise noted, all command chronologies cited in this text are housed at the Gray Research Center, Quantico, VA; Sattler intvw; Natonski intvw; Holbert intvw.

21. Sattler and Wilson, "Operation Al Fajr."

22. Ibid.

23. Intvw with Capt Jeffrey S. McCormack, 6 January 2005 (MCHC, Quantico, VA).

24. Ibid.

25. Sattler intvw; LtGen Richard F. Natonski brief, 3 April 2008 (MCHC, Quantico, VA); Sattler and Wilson, "Operation Al Fajr"; Wright and Reese, *On Point II*, 20; Matt M. Matthews, *Operation Al Fajr: A Study in Army and Marine Corps Joint Operations* (Ft. Leavenworth, KS: Combat Studies Institute Press, 2006), 33.

26. Natonski brief; Natonski comments.

27. Sattler and Wilson, "Operation Al Fajr"; Natonski brief.

28. Sattler intvw; Natonski brief; Sattler and Wilson, "Operation Al Fajr"; Wright and Reese, *On Point II*, 20; Matthews, *Operation Al Fajr*, 13–34.

29. Sattler intvw; Natonski brief; Sattler and Wilson, "Operation Al Fajr"; Wright and Reese, *On Point II*, 20; Matthews, *Operation Al Fajr*, 13–34; Natonski comments.

30. Natonski intvw.

31. Sattler and Wilson, "Operation Al Fajr."

32. LtCol Gary A. Kling intvw, 7 June 2005 (MCHC, Quantico, VA); Sattler intvw. Further information on close air support in Fallujah can be found in Maj Fred H. Allison, "Close Air Support: A Core Contributor to Successful Integrated Operations in Fallujah," *Marine Corps Gazette* 92, no. 10 (2008): 70–76.

33. BGen Dennis J. Hejlik intvw, 5 January 2005 (MCHC, Quantico, VA); Sattler intvw; Natonski comments, DeFrancisci comments.

34. Sattler intvw.

35. Ibid.

36. Ibid.

37. Natonski comments.

38. Ibid.

39. Capt Jason P. Schauble intvw, 16 November 2004 (MCHC, Quantico, VA).

40. John R. Ballard, *Fighting for Fallujah: A New Dawn for Iraq* (Westport, CT: Praeger Security International, 2006), 49.

41. Ballard, *Fighting for Fallujah*, 50.

42. Capt Thomas M. Tennant intvw, 6 February 2005 (MCHC, Quantico, VA).

43. Natonski brief; Natonski intvw; "Close Air Support Mission Strikes Anti-Iraqi Forces in Fallujah," *MNF–I News*, 3 November 2004, http://www.globalsecurity.org/military/library/news /2004/11/mil–041103–mnfi–mnci01.htm; "Fallujah-Ramadi Operations Update," *MNF–I News*, 3 November 2004, http://www.globalsecurity.org/military/library/news/2004/11/mil–041103–mnfi–mnci02.htm; "Fallujah–Ramadi Operations Update," *MNF–I News*, 4 November 2004, http://www.globalsecurity.org/military/library/news/2004/11/mil–041104–mnfi–mnci01.htm; "U.S. Forces Attack Al-Fallujah Targets," *Radio Free Europe/Radio Liberty*, 4 November 2004, http://www.globalsecurity.org/military/library/news/2004/11/mil–041104–rferl01.htm; "Fallujah-Ramadi, 5 Nov, Operations Update," *MNF–I News*, 5 November 2004, http://www.globalsecurity.org/military/library/news/2004/11/mil–041105–mnfi–mnci01.htm; "Fallujah–Ramadi Operations Update," *MNF–I News*, 6 November 2004, http://www.globalsecurity.org/military/library/news/2004/11/mil–041106–mnfi–mnci03.htm; "ISF, Marines Capture Insurgents in Northern Babil," *MNF–I News*, 5 November 2004, http://www.globalsecurity.org/military/library/news/2004/11/mil–041106–mnfi–mnci01.htm.

44. LtCol Myles M. Miyamasu intvw, 14 December 2004 (MCHC, Quantico, VA).

45. Ibid.

46. Kendal D. Gott and Jennifer Lindsey, eds., *Eyewitness to War, Volume I: The US Army in Operation AL FAJR: An Oral History* (Ft. Leavenworth, KS: Combat Studies Institute Press, 2006), 32.

47. Maj Travis L. Homiak intvw, 4 January 2005 (MCHC, Quantico, VA); Sattler and Wilson, "Operation Al Fajr."

48. Sattler intvw; Natonski brief; Sattler and Wilson, "Operation Al Fajr."

49. Gott and Lindsey, *Eyewitness to War, vol. I: The US Army in Operation AL FAJR: An Oral History* (Ft. Leavenworth, KS:

Combat Studies Institute Press, 2006), 33–34, 40–41; Sattler and Wilson, "Operation Al Fajr."

50. "Fallujah–Ramadi Operations Update," *MNF–I News*, 7 November 2004, http://www.globalsecurity.org/military /library/news/2004/11/mil–041107–mnfi–mnci01.htm; Natonski intvw; Natonski comments.

51. Col Craig Tucker intvw, 11 August 2006 (MCHC, Quantico, VA).

52. Named for John Wayne's character in the film *The Sands of Iwo Jima*, Sgt John M. Stryker, and not for the Stryker light armored vehicle.

53. Task Force Stryker After Action Report (MCHC, Quantico, VA); LtCol Todd Desgrosseilliers review comments (MCHC, Quantico, VA); Richard S. Lowry, *New Dawn: The Battles for Fallujah* (New York: Savas Beatie, 2010), 86.

54. LtCol Stephen R. Dinauer intvw, 31 January 2005 (MCHC, Quantico, VA); Sattler and Wilson, "Operation Al Fajr"; LtCol Todd Desgrosseilliers comments on draft MS (MCHC, Quantico, VA); Gott and Lindsey, *Eyewitness to War, vol. I*, 55.

55. LtCol John R. Way intvw with LtCol Gary S. Patton, 12 March 2005 (MCHC, Quantico, VA); Sattler and Wilson, "Operation Al Fajr"; Ballard, *Fighting for Fallujah*, 58; Doug Sample, "Iraqi Prime Minister Issues State of Emergency Throughout Country," American Forces Press Service, 7 November 2004, http://www.globalsecurity.org/military /library/news/2004/11/mil–041107–afps01.htm; "Iraq Wrap: Insurgents Launch Attacks Across Iraq as U.S. Prepares for Fallujah Battle," *Voice of America*, 7 November 2004, http://www.globalsecurity.org/military/library/news/2004/11 /mil–041107–327b8b43.htm.

56. Sattler and Wilson, "Operation Al Fajr"; Natonski brief; Natonski comments; Capt James T. Cobb, 1stLt Christopher A. LaCour, and SFC William H. Hight, "TF 2-2 in FSE AAR: Indirect Fires in the Battle of Fallujah," *Field Artillery*, March–April 2005, 23; LtCol Kiel R. Gentry, "Regimental Combat Team 1 Fires in the Battle of Fallujah," *Field Artillery*, November–December 2005, 26.

57. Capt Scott M. Conway intvw, 16 June 2005 (MCHC, Quantico, VA).

58. Dinauer intvw; Task Force Wolfpack After Action brief, 15 December 2004; Richard S. Lowry, *New Dawn: The Battles for Fallujah* (New York: Savas Beatie, 2010), 78–79.

59. Estes, *Into the Fray*, 65-66; Sattler and Wilson, "Operation Al Fajr."

60. Intvw with Maj David C. Morris, 16 November 2004 (MCHC, Quantico, VA); Schauble intvw; Homiak intvw; Natonski comments.

61. Sattler and Wilson, "Operation Al Fajr"; Natonski brief.

62. LtCol Michael Ramos intvw, 9 February 2005 (MCHC, Quantico, VA).

63. Sattler and Wilson, "Operation Al Fajr."

64. Sattler intvw; Natonski brief; Sattler and Wilson, "Operation Al Fajr."

65. Natonski intvw.

66. 1stLt John Flanagan intvw, 19 November 2004 (MCHC, Quantico, VA); LCpl Justin A. Boswood intvw, 21 October 2005 (MCHC, Quantico, VA).

67. Capt Jay Garcia intvw, 6 February 2005 (MCHC,Quantico, VA); LtCol Peter A. Newell intvw, 21 November 2004 (MCHC, Quantico, VA).

68. Gott and Lindsey, *Eyewitness to War, vol. I*, 143.

69. Capt Andrew J. McNulty intvw, 22 November 2004 (MCHC, Quantico, VA); Desgrosseilliers intvw, 20 December 2004 (MCHC, Quantico, VA); Desgrosseilliers comments.

70. Capt Robert J. Bodisch intvw, 17 December 2004 (MCHC, Quantico, VA).

71. Maj Christeon Griffin intvw, 5 October 2005 (MCHC, Quantico, VA).

72. Col Craig Tucker intvw.

73. Gott and Lindsey, *Eyewitness to War, vol. I*, 91.

74. Ibid., 92–93.

75. Maj Travis L. Homiak intvw; Dinauer intvw; Task Force Wolfpack After Action Brief; Gott and Lindsey, *Eyewitness to War, vol. I*, 33–34, 43.

76. Griffin intvw; LtCol John R. Way intvw with Col Michael A. Shupp, 27 May 2005, (MCHC, Quantico, VA); Griffin intvw; Gott and Lindsey, *Eyewitness to War, vol. I*, 55–57; Natonski comments.

77. Bodisch intvw.

78. Desgrosseilliers intvw; McNulty intvw.

79. Shupp intvw.

80. Ibid.; Bodisch intvw; Gott and Lindsey, *Eyewitness to War, vol. I*, 202; Kendall D. Gott and Jennifer Lindsey, eds., *Eyewitness to War, vol. II: The US Army in Operation AL FAJR: An Oral History* (Ft. Leavenworth, KS: Combat Studies Institute, 2006), 73.

81. Gott and Lindsey, *Eyewitness to War, vol. I*, 202.

82. Boswood intvw.

83. Gott and Lindsey, *Eyewitness to War, vol. I*, 56.

84. Shupp intvw; Gott and Lindsey, *Eyewitness to War, vol. I*, 56, 203, 270.

85. Gott and Lindsey, *Eyewitness to War, vol. I,* 270.

86. Ibid., 56.

87. Shupp intvw; Bodisch, intvw; Capt Timothy Jent intvw, 7 January 2005 (MCHC, Quantico, VA); Gott and Lindsey, *Eyewitness to War, vol. I,* 56, 203. 270; Patrick K. O'Donnell, *We Were One: Shoulder to Shoulder with the Marines Who Took Fallujah* (Cambridge, MA: Da Capo, 2006), 76–77.

88. Tucker intvw.

89. Gott and Lindsey, *Eyewitness to War, vol. I,* 93, 97.

90. Newell intvw.

91. Tucker intvw.

92. Gott and Lindsey, *Eyewitness to War, vol. I,* 146.

93. Maj Mark E. Winn intvw, 18 November 2004 (MCHC, Quantico, VA); 1stLt Christopher Conner intvw, 17 November 2004 (MCHC, Quantico, VA); Morris intvw 16 November 2004 (MCHC, Quantico, VA); Schauble intvw; Capt Theodore C. Bethea intvw, 17 November 2004 (MCHC, Quantico, VA).

94. Conner, intvw; Maj Theodore Bethea comments on draft MS (MCHC, Quantico, VA).

95. Bethea intvw; Conner intvw; Tucker intvw; Winn intvw; Bethea comments.

96. Capt Michael Stroud intvw, 17 November 2004 (MCHC, Quantico, VA).

97. Conner intvw.

98. Bethea comments.

99. Tennant intvw.

100. Tennant intvw; Ramos intvw; Garcia intvw; Newell intvw.

101. LtCol John R. Way intvw with Capt Brian T. Mulvihil, 26 November 2005 (MCHC, Quantico, VA); Ramos intvw; Tennant intvw.

102. Tennant intvw.

103. Gott and Lindsey, *Eyewitness to War, vol. I,* 121.

104. Ibid.

105. Ibid., 270–71.

106. LtCol Eduardo Bitanga comments on draft manuscript (MCHC, Quantico, VA).

107. Desgrosseilliers intvw; McNulty intvw; Lowry, *New Dawn,* 131, 171.

108. Desgrosseilliers intvw.

109. Griffin intvw; Jent intvw.

110. Ibid.

111. Ibid.

112. Ibid.; Bodisch intvw.

113. O'Donnell, *We Were One,* 85–99.

114. McNulty intvw; M. P. Del Palazzo, "Marine Tanks: The Corps' Indispensable Asset" (Contemporary Issues Paper, Expeditionary Warfare School, Marine Corps University, 16 December 2005), 5, 8; Ron Synovitz, "Iraq: U.S. Military Says One-Third of Al-Fallujah Under Its Control," *Radio Free Europe/Radio Liberty,* 9 November 2004, http://www.globalsecurity.org/military/library/news/2004/11/mil-041109-rferl04.htm.

115. Gott and Lindsey, *Eyewitness to War, vol. I,* 203.

116. McNulty intvw.

117. Desgrosseilliers intvw; McNulty intvw.

118. Bitanga comments; Ned Parker and Patrick Baz, "City of Death's Secret Torture Rooms Revealed," Independent Online, 18 November 2004, http://www.iol.co.za/news/world/city-of-death-s-secret-torture-rooms-revealed-1.227266?ot=inmsa.ArticlePrintPageLayout.ot.

119. Bodisch intvw.

120. Griffin intvw; Jent intvw; Lt John Zaal intvw, 8 January 2005 (MCHC, Quantico, VA); 1st Lt Michael Deland intvw, 8 January 2005 (MCHC, Quantico, VA); Gott and Lindsey, *Eyewitness to War, vol. I,* 122; Gott and Lindsey, *Eyewitness to War, vol. II,* 130.

121. Desgrosseilliers intvw; McNulty intvw; Gott and Lindsey, *Eyewitness to War, vol. I,* 123–24; Gott and Lindsey, *Eyewitness to War, vol. II,* 74–75.

122. Gott and Lindsey, *Eyewitness to War, vol. II,* 75.

123. Gott and Lindsey, *Eyewitness to War, vol. I,* 124; Sattler and Wilson, "Operation Al Fajr."

124. Gott and Lindsey, *Eyewitness to War, vol. II,* 30–31.

125. Ibid., 30.

126. Ibid., 31.

127. Ibid., 154.

128. Tennant intvw.

129. Garcia intvw.

130. Ramos intvw; Garcia intvw; Tennant intvw.

131. Mulvihill intvw.

132. Tennant intvw.

133. Ibid.

134. Morris intvw; Schauble intvw; Tucker intvw; Gary Livingston, *Fallujah, with Honor: First Battalion, Eighth Marine's Role in Operation Phantom Fury* (North Topsail Beach, NC: Caisson Press, 2006), 72–77.

135. Conner intvw.

136. Winn intvw.

137. Bethea comments; Capt Read M. Omohundro comments on draft MS (MCHC, Quantico, VA).

138. Tucker intvw; Bethea comments.

139. Tucker intvw; Bethea intvw; "Forces Retake Key Civic Centers In Fallujah," Central Command news release, 10 November 2004, http://www.globalsecurity.org/military/library/news /2004/11/mil–041110–centcom02.htm.

140. Tucker intvw; Bethea intvw; "Forces Retake Key Civic Centers In Fallujah," Central Command news release.

141. Morris intvw.

142. Mulvihill intvw.

143. Tennant intvw.

144. Ibid.

145. Mulvihill intvw.

146. Gott and Lindsey, *Eyewitness to War, vol. I,* 31, 302–3; Gott, *Eyewitness to War, vol. II,* 32, 156–57.

147. Gott and Lindsey, *Eyewitness to War, vol. I,* 303.

148. Ibid., 98; Gott and Lindsey, *Eyewitness to War, vol. II,* 32–33; Newell intvw.

149. Ramos intvw.

150. Garcia intvw.

151. Tennant intvw.

152. Ramos intvw.

153. Mulvihill intvw.

154. Tennant intvw; Garcia intvw; Conner intvw; Desgrosseilliers intvw; Griffin intvw; Tennant intvw; Gott and Lindsey, *Eyewitness to War, vol. I,* 97.

155. Buhl intwv.

156. Gott and Lindsey, *Eyewitness to War, vol. II,* 75.

157. Ibid., 131.

158. Buhl intwv; 1stSgt Robert C. Bayne intvw, 9 October 2007 (MCHC, Quantico, VA); 1stLt Jason E. Mansel intvw, 9 February 2005 (MCHC, Quantico, VA).

159. 1stLt John Jacobs intvw, 7 January 2005 (MCHC, Quantico, VA).

160. Buhl intwv.

161. Griffin intvw.

162. O'Donnell, *We Were One,* 111–14; Maj Jeffrey McCormack comments on draft MS (MCHC, Quantico, VA).

163. Buhl intvw; McNulty intvw, 22 November 2004.

164. McNulty intvw, 22 November 2004; Bourgeois intvw, 23 November 2004 (MCHC, Quantico, VA).

165. Bitanga comments.

166. LtCol Patrick J. Malay intvw, 19 November 2004 (MCHC, Quantico, VA).

167. McNulty intvw, 22 November 2004; Shupp intvw; Bourgeois intvw.

168. Bourgeois intvw.

169. McNulty intvw, 22 November 2004.

170. Gott and Lindsey, *Eyewitness to War, vol. II,* 131.

171. Ibid., 124.

172. Shupp intvw.

173. Shupp intvw; Gott and Lindsey, *Eyewitness to War, vol. I,* 58, 204, 272–73; Desgrosseilliers intvw.

174. Jent intvw; Jacobs intvw.

175. Jent intvw; Jacobs intvw; Maj Andrew J. McNulty intvw, 1 April 2001 (MCHC, Quantico, VA); Bourgeois intvw; Camp, *Operation Phantom Fury,* 221; Lowry, *New Dawn,* 143–45.

176. McNulty intvw, 22 November 2004; McNulty intvw, 1 April 2001.

177. Ibid.

178. Ibid.

179. Ibid.

180. Bitanga comments.

181. Flanagan intvw; LtCol Gareth F. Brandl intvw, 18 November 2004 (MCHC, Quantico, VA); Winn intvw.

182. Flanagan intvw; Schauble intvw; Livingston, *Fallujah, with Honor,* 148–49; Central Command, "Terrorists Use Mosque To Fire Upon Forces," news release, 10 November 2004, http://www.globalsecurity.org/military/library/news /2004/11/mil–041110–centcom01.htm.

183. Tennant intvw; Garcia intvw.

184. Tennant intvw.

185. Garcia intvw; Tennant intvw.

186. Mulvihill intvw

187. Tucker intvw; Sattler and Wilson, "Operation Al Fajr"; Gott and Lindsey, *Eyewitness to War, vol. I*, 256–59; Gott and Lindsey, *Eyewitness to War, vol. II*, 5–6, 32–33, 260–69; SSgt David Bellavia Silver Star Citation for Actions on 10 November 2004, Lowry, *New Dawn*, 306.

188. Flanagan intvw; Bethea intvw; Stroud intvw; Livingston, *Fallujah, with Honor*, 148–49; Central Command, "Terrorists Use Mosque To Fire Upon Forces."

189. Bethea intvw; Morris intvw; Conner intvw.

190. Bethea comments.

191. Bethea intvw; Morris intvw; Schauble intvw; Livingston, *Fallujah, with Honor*, 150–51.

192. Homiak intvw; Gott and Lindsey, *Eyewitness to War, vol. I*, 33.

193. LtCol John R. Way intvw with Capt Scott M. Conway, 16 June 2005 (MCHC, Quantico, VA).

194. LtCol Stephen R. Dinauer comments on draft MS (MCHC, Quantico, VA).

195. Conway intvw; Task Force Wolfpack After Action brief; Col Dinauer comments.

196. Sattler and Wilson, "Operation Al Fajr"; Shupp intvw; Winslow, *Eyewitness to Operation Al Fajr*.

197. Gott and Lindsey, *Eyewitness to War, vol. I*, 101–2.

198. Griffin intvw; Deland intvw; Buhl intwv; Gott and Lindsey, *Eyewitness to War, vol. I*, 124; O'Donnell, *We Were One*, 117–19; "Operation Al Fajr Roll Up" Briefing, Multi National Force-Iraq, 28 November 2004, www.globalsecurity.org/military/library/report/.../d20041203 entire.ppt; Joe Bauman and Geoffrey Fattah "Hassoun ID Discovered: Fallujah Find Could Strengthen Utahn's Claim," *Desert News*, 18 November 2004, http://www.deseretnews .com/article /595106220/Hassoun–ID–discovered.html.

199. O'Donnell, *We Were One*, 120–23.

200. Bitanga comments.

201. Ibid.; "French hostages' Driver Found in Falluja," *Associated Press*, 12 November 2004, http://www.guardian.co.uk/media/2004/nov/12/Iraqandthem edia.pressandpublishing.

202. McNulty intvw.

203. Bourgeois intvw.

204. Griffin intvw; Deland intvw; Profile of Justin D. McLeese at the website of the Department of Defense, http://ourmilitaryheroes.defense.gov/profiles/mcleeseJ.html.

205. Bethea intvw; Conner intvw; Schauble intvw; Morris intvw.

206. Conner intvw.

207. Brandl intvw; Schauble intvw; Morris intvw; Bethea intvw; Conner intvw.

208. Livingston, *Fallujah, with Honor*, 175–82.

209. Stroud intvw; Brandl intvw.

210. Brandl intvw.

211. Flanagan intvw.

212. Gott and Lindsey, *Eyewitness to War, vol. I*, 101–2.

213. Garcia intvw.

214. Tennant intvw.

215. Natonski intvw; LtCol John R. Ballard intvw, 11 December 2004 (MCHC, Quantico, VA); GySgt Duanne Walters intvw, 6 January 2005 (MCHC, Quantico, VA); Natonski comments.

216. Lowry, *New Dawn*, 160–61.

217. Jent intvw; Deland intvw; Gott and Lindsey, *Eyewitness to War, vol. II*, 124, 131; McCormack comments.

218. Gott and Lindsay, *Eyewitness to War, vol. II*, 76.

219. Ibid., 77.

220. Ibid.

221. Gott and Lindsey, *Eyewitness to War, vol. I*, 85.

222. Flanagan intvw; Stroud intvw; Gott and Lindsey, *Eyewitness to War, vol. I*, 101–2; Livingston, *Fallujah, with Honor*, 199–202.

223. Gott and Lindsey, *Eyewitness to War, vol. II*, 35.

224. Gott and Lindsey, *Eyewitness to War, vol. I*, 101.

225. Ibid., 102–3.

226. Flanagan intvw; Livingston, *Fallujah, with Honor*, 106, 199–202, 204–5.

227. Morris intvw; Schauble intvw.

228. Morris intvw.

229. Gott and Lindsey, *Eyewitness to War, vol. II*, 131–32.

230. Ibid., 132.

231. Ibid., 76, 133; Gott and Lindsey, *Eyewitness to War, vol. I*, 275.

232. Griffin intvw; Deland intvw; Jent intvw; Buhl intwv; Bodisch intvw; Gott and Lindsey, *Eyewitness to War, vol. I*, 62.

233. Boswood intvw.

234. McCormack intvw; Gott and Lindsey, *Eyewitness to War, vol. I*, 62.

235. McCormack intvw.

236. Deland intvw.

237. Ballard, *Fighting for Fallujah*, 64.

238. McCormack intvw; Boswood intvw; McCormack Comments.

239. Flanagan intvw; Livingston, *Fallujah, with Honor*, 204–5.

240. Bethea intvw.

241. Livingston, *Fallujah, with Honor*, 204–5.

242. Garcia intvw; Shupp intvw; Natonski intvw; Sattler and Wilson, "Operation Al Fajr"; Winslow, *Eyewitness to Operation Al Fajr*; Ballard, *Fighting for Fallujah*, 65, 73.

243. Jent intvw; Griffin intvw; Gott and Lindsey, *Eyewitness to War, vol. I*, 62.

244. Gott and Lindsey, *Eyewitness to War, vol. I*, 102–3.

245. Ibid.

246. Gott and Lindsey, *Eyewitness to War, vol. II*, 36–37, 64–55; McCormack comments.

247. Intvw with Maj Lawrence K. Hussey, 19 November 2004 (MCHC, Quantico, VA); Flanagan intvw.

248. Winslow, *Eyewitness to Operation Al Fajr*.

249. Natonski brief.

250. Hussey intvw.

251. Natonski comments.

252. Gott and Lindsey, *Eyewitness to War, vol. I*, 206.

253. Natonski brief; Sattler and Wilson, "Operation Al Fajr."

254. Jent intvw; Griffin intvw.

255. Jent intvw.

256. Jent intvw; Jacobs intvw; Boswood intvw; "Former Marine Receives Navy Cross for Heroism," 4 August 2006, http://www.defense.gov/home/faceofdefense/fod/2006 –08/f20060804a.html.

257. Jacobs intvw.

258. Buhl intwv; Jacobs intvw.

259. Jent intvw.

260. Griffin intvw; Deland intvw; Holbert intvw; McCormack comments; Natonski comments.

261. Gott and Lindsey, *Eyewitness to War, vol. II*, 135.

262. Natonski brief.

263. Gott and Lindsey, *Eyewitness to War vol. I*, 102–3; Gott and Lindsey, *Eyewitness to War, vol. II*, 37.

264. Bethea comments.

265. Ibid.

266. Bourgeois intvw; Winslow, *Eyewitness to Operation Al Fajr*; West, *No True Glory*, 307; Barrie McKenna, "Marines Mop Up in Fallujah," *Globe and Mail*, 14 November 2004, http://www.leatherneck.com/forums/showthread.php?t=1748 9; "Mutilated Blonde Corpse Found," News 24, 14 November 2004, http://www.news24.com/World/Archives/IraqiDossier /Mutilated–blonde–corpse–found–20041114; "Family Heartbreak Over Hassan fate," CNN.com, http://www.cnn .com/2004/WORLD/meast/11/16/iraq.hassan/index.html; Dexter Filkins and Lizette Alvarez, "Kidnappers Seize a Relief Official Working in Iraq," *The New York Times*, 20 October 2004, http://www.nytimes.com/2004/10/20/international /middleeast/20iraq.html?_r=1.

267. McNulty intvw.

268. Tennant intvw.

269. Flanagan intvw; Livingston, *Fallujah, with Honor*, 206.

270. Natonski brief.

271. Task Force Wolfpack After Action brief; Winslow, *Eyewitness to Operation Al Fajr*; McKenna, "Marines Mop Up in Fallujah."

272. Gott and Lindsey, *Eyewitness to War, vol. I*, 206.

273. Ibid., 104.

274. Ibid.; Greg Lamotte, "New Fighting Erupts in Iraq," Voice of America, 14 November 2004, http://www.globalsecurity.org/military/library/news/2004/11 /mil––041114–2c7ba06d.htm; Ron Synovitz, "Iraq: U.S. Forces Continue 'Clearing Operations' In Al-Fallujah," Radio Free Europe/Radio Liberty, 15Nov04,http://www.rferl.org /content/article/1055888.html.

275. Brandl intvw; Gott and Lindsey, *Eyewitness to War, vol. II*, 136; Livingston, *Fallujah, with Honor*, 216.

276. Flanagan intvw.

277. Associated Press, "In the Wake of Fallujah Battle, Clearing the Dead," 16 November 2004, http://www.nbcnews .com/id/6504719/ns/world_news-mideast_n_africa/t/wake -fallujah-battle-clearing-dead/#.UhdhObyAHOE.

278. McNulty intvw; Bourgeois intvw; Desgrosseilliers intvw; I MEF & MNC–I Effects Exploitation Team, "Telling the Fallujah Story to the World" (Third cut) (brief, 20 November 2004), http://www2.nationalreview.com/document /document_20041129_fallujah.pdf; Miguel A. Carrasco Jr., "Marines Reopen Fallujah Bridge," *Marine Corps News*, 15 November 2004, http://www.globalsecurity.org/military /library/news /2004/11/mil–041120–usmc01.htm; Miguel A. Carrasco Jr., "U.S. Marines with K-9s Search for Weapons," *Marine Corps News*, 14 November 2004,

http://www.globalsecurity.org/military/library/news/2004/11/mil–041119–usmc01.htm.

279. Miyamasu intvw; Natonski brief; Task Force Wolfpack After Action brief; Gott and Lindsey, *Eyewitness to War, vol. I*, 45; "Mosul Stable, Stryker Battalion Rejoins Brigade," *Stryker Brigade News*, 15 November 2004, http://www.strykernews.com/archives/2004/11/15/mosul_stable_stryker_battalion_rejoins_brigade.html#.

280. Synovitz, "Iraq: U.S. Forces Continue 'Clearing Operations.' "

281. Office of the Assistant Secretary of Defense, "Operational Update on Fallujah, Iraq," transcript, 15 November 2004, http://www.globalsecurity.org/military/library/news/2004/11/mil-041115-dod01.htm.

282. "U.S. Military Says Al-Fallujah Occupied," *Radio Free Europe/Radio Liberty*, 14 November 2004, http://www.globalsecurity.org/military/library/news/2004/11/mil–041114–rferl01.htm.

283. Synovitz, "Iraq: U.S. Forces Continue 'Clearing Operations.' "

284. Jacobs intvw; Jent intvw; Deland intvw; McNulty intvw; Bourgeois intvw; O'Donnell, *We Were One*, 177, 157–8.

285. Bourgeois intvw.

286. Ibid.

287. Ibid.

288. Gott and Lindsey, *Eyewitness to War, vol. I*, 105.

289. Ibid., 251.

290. Flanagan intvw; Stroud intvw.

291. Flanagan intvw.

292. Rafael Peralta Navy Cross Citation; Natonski comments.

293. Homiak intvw; Miyamasu intvw; Task Force Wolfpack After Action brief; Centcom, "Iraqi Army Continues Operations in Fallujah" press release, 16 November 2004, http://www.globalsecurity.org/military/library/news/2004/11/mil–041116–centcom01.htm; "Fighting Continues In Al-Fallujah, Flares In Ba'qubah," *Radio Free Europe/Radio Liberty*, 15 November 2004, http://www.rferl.org/content/article/1055890.html.

294. Griffin intvw; Jent intvw; Deland intvw; Luis R. Agostini, "Marines Assist Iraqis Recover Remains of Fallujah Conflict," *Marine Corps News*, 17 November 2004, http://www.globalsecurity.org/military/library/news/2004/11/mil–041119–usmc04.htm.

295. Gott and Lindsey, *Eyewitness to War, vol. I*, 105.

296. Ibid., 253.

297. Flanagan intvw.

298. Ibid.

299. Ibid.

300. Griffin intvw; Ballard, *Fighting for Fallujah*, 74; Luis R. Agostini, "Marines Reopen Iraqi Supply Lanes Following Fallujah Battle," *Marine Corps News*, 16 November 2004, http://www.globalsecurity.org/military/library/news/2004/11/mil–041119–usmc03.htm

301. Gott and Lindsey, *Eyewitness to War, vol. I*, 105.

302. Ibid., 45.

303. Jent intvw; Jacobs intvw.

304. Ibid.

305. Jacobs intvw.

306. Ibid.

307. Ibid.

308. Jent intvw; Jacobs intvw; O'Donnell, *We Were One*, 169–70; McCormack comments.

309. Stroud intvw; Gott and Lindsey, *Eyewitness to War, vol. I*, 105.

310. Bethea intvw.

311. Brandl intvw.

312. RCT-1 ComdC, November 2004; DeFrancisci comments; Ballard, *Fighting for Fallujah*, 74; Ballard intvw; John R. Ballard, "Lessons learned from Operation Al Fajr: The Liberation of Fallujah" (paper presented at 10th Annual Command and Control Research and Technology Symposium, McLean, VA, 2005); Winslow, *Eyewitness to Operation Al Fajr*.

313. Griffin intvw.

314. Jacobs intvw; Griffin intvw.

315. Griffin intvw.

316. Gott and Lindsey, *Eyewitness to War, vol. I*, 105.

317. Livingston, *Fallujah, with Honor*, 224.

318. Stroud intvw.

319. Task Force Wolfpack After Action brief.

320. O'Donnell, *We Were One*, 76–77.

321. Jacobs intvw.

322. Jent intvw.

323. Gott and Lindsey, *Eyewitness to War, vol. I*, 105; Livingston, *Fallujah, with Honor*, 224–27.

324. Bethea comments.

325. Sattler intvw; DeFrancisci comments.

326. Natonski intvw.

327. Homiak, intvw; Miyamasu intvw; Natonski intvw; Gott and Lindsey, *Eyewitness to War, vol. I*, 37; "Marine Unit Continues Offensive Operations in Jabella," *Central Command News*, 23 November 2004, http://www.globalsecurity.org/military/library/news/2004/11/mil-041123-centcom02.htm.

328. Sattler intvw; Natonski intvw.

329. Anne Barnard, "Returning Fallujans Will Face Clampdown," *Boston Globe*, 5 December 2004; Scott Peterson, "U.S. Smoothes Way in Fallujah for Muslim Relief Agency," *Christian Science Monitor*, 29 November 2004.

330. Sattler intvw; Ballard, *Fighting for Fallujah*, 77–80.

331. DeFrancisci comments.

332. Sattler and Wilson, "Operation Al Fajr"; Ballard, *Fighting for Fallujah*, 81; Steven Komarow, "Fallujans Reluctant to Go Home, Despite Aid," *USA Today*, 6 January 2005; Desgrosseilliers comments.

333. DeFrancisci comments; "Fallujah's Critical Infrastructure Assessed," *MNF–I News*, 17 December 2004, http://www.globalsecurity.org/military/library/news/2004/12/mil-041217-mnfi-mnci02.htm.

334. Ballard intvw; Shupp intvw; Buhl intwv.

335. McNulty intvw; Maj Desgrossielliers Silver Star Citation for Action 12–23 December 2004, Lowry, *New Dawn*, 311.

336. McNulty intvw.

337. Ibid.

338. Ibid.

339. Ibid.

340. Ibid.

341. Ibid.

342. Ibid.

343. Ibid.

344. Hejlik intvw; Shupp intvw; Ballard, *Fighting for Fallujah*, 82–83.

345. Sattler intvw; Natonski, intvw; Hejlik intvw; "Iraqis, U.S. Forces Support Residents' Return To Fallujah," *Centcom News*, 23 November 2004, http://www.globalsecurity.org/military/library/news/2004/12/mil-041224-centcom01.htm; DeFrancisci comments.

346. LCpl David Garcia intvw, 11 December 2004 (MCHC, Quantico, VA); 1stLt Sarah Hope intvw, 31 January 2005 (MCHC, Quantico, VA); Maj Robert Belknap II intvw, 7 January 2005 (MCHC, Quantico, VA).

347. "Iraqis, U.S. Forces Support Residents' Return To Fallujah."

348. Task Force Stryker and Task Force Bruno After Action Report; Maj Desgrossiellier's Silver Star Citation.

349. Shupp intvw.

350. Sattler and Wilson, "Operation Al Fajr"; Ballard, *Fighting for Fallujah*, 89, 90–92; Scott Peterson, "Fallujans Welcome Security, Await Electricity," *Christian Science Monitor*, 8 February 2005, 1; DeFrancisci comments.

351. Malkasian, "Signaling Resolve: Democratization and the First Battle of Fallujah," 423–52.

352. These numbers are drawn from Wright and Reese, *On Point II*, 357, which largely utilize figures given to the authors by General Natonski. Nevertheless, figures still vary across different sources. West gives a number of 70 American killed in action and 609 wounded. Ricks's figures are 54 American dead and 425 wounded, 8 Iraqi soldiers killed, and 43 Iraqi soldiers wounded. The I Marine Expeditionary Force Summary of Action gives lower numbers for insurgent casualties, estimating that the Coalition took over 1,000 prisoners and killed a similar number. Estes only lists Marine losses, and indicates they were 70 killed in action, 651 wounded. See West, *No True Glory*, 316; Ricks, *Fiasco*, 400; I Marine Expeditionary Force Summary of Action in *U.S. Marines in Iraq, 2004–2008: Anthology and Annotated Bibliography*, 88; Estes, *Into the Fray*, 78.

About the Authors and Acknowledgments

This battle study is a portion of a larger manuscript dealing with events in Iraq in 2004–5. This version was published to document events of that period for the benefit of Marine students, educators, and trainers. A more definitive account was provided by the History Division's monograph *U.S. Marines in Iraq, 2004–2005: Into the Fray* by Lieutenant Colonel (Ret) Kenneth W. Estes. Division director Dr. Charles P. Neimeyer and chief historian Charles D. Melson provided needed insights and sponsorship. Senior editors Kenneth H. Williams and Angela J. Anderson took charge of the editing and design process. The project could not have been completed without the needed skills of historian Dr. Nicholas Schlosser, editorial assistant Wanda J. Renfrow, manuscript editor Andrea Connell, and graphic design by Vincent J. Martinez.

It was compiled and written by members of the History Division's individual mobilization augmentees the field historians. These included Major Stephen J. Winslow who witnessed the Battle of Fallujah with Regimental Combat Team 1 in 2004. Master Gunnery Sergeant Robert A. Yarnall assembled the records and completed a draft while on duty from 2006 to 2008. Chief Warrant Officer-4 Timothy S. McWilliams, also a Fallujah participant and a coeditor of the Marine Corps University Press two-volume *Al-Anbar Awakening*, completed the project in 2011. It was reviewed by selected participants including Lieutenant General Richard F. Natonski. It depended in large part on the field interviews given by those who fought the battle.

History Division
United States Marine Corps
Quantico, VA
2014
PCN 10600009200